D1273412

Lavery Library

St. John Fisher
College
Rochester, New York

THE PUERTO RICAN JOURNEY

New York's Newest Migrants

PUBLICATIONS OF THE BUREAU OF APPLIED SOCIAL RESEARCH, COLUMBIA UNIVERSITY

Paul F. Lazarsfeld
Editor

MASS PERSUASION
The Social Psychology of a War Bond Drive

by Robert K. Merton

SAY IT WITH FIGURES

by Hans Zeisel

COMMUNICATIONS RESEARCH 1948–1949

Edited by Paul F. Lazarsfeld
and Frank N. Stanton

THE PUERTO RICAN JOURNEY
New York's Newest Migrants

by C. Wright Mills,
Clarence Senior and Rose Kohn Goldsen

The Puerto Rican Journey

New York's Newest Migrants

BY

C. WRIGHT MILLS
CLARENCE SENIOR
ROSE KOHN GOLDSEN

HARPER & BROTHERS PUBLISHERS

NEW YORK

THE PUERTO RICAN JOURNEY

Contents

Preface

Aim

THIS is a report on the Puerto Rican migration to New York City, and of the migrants' colonies in Spanish Harlem and in the Morrisania area of the Bronx. It begins on the island and ends with the aspirations of the Puerto Ricans in New York City. We try to tell who the migrants are and why they came; how they compare with their compatriots who remain at home; what their journey to the continent means in their occupational and income as well as life stories; what kind of social world they inhabit in New York, and how that world compares with the kind of world New York has been for previous migrants; what seem to be their solidarities and their conflicts with other ethnic and racial groups in the city of New York; what is meant by "adaptation" for a group at this level of living, and how the Puerto Ricans are involved in this process in the middle of the twentieth century.

As a document of larger human significance, our report must speak for itself; we want to say only that we are aware that no study of this kind can capture the full human meaning of the journey from Puerto Rico to New York City and of the splendors and miseries of the people who make it. Confronted with a subject as alive, deep, and varied as a people on the move, we have had to rely largely on the collective and somewhat distant experience which statistical research offers, catching it in bits and pieces which we then try to fit together into some sort of understandable pattern.

As an academic contribution, our work may be of some value value in three fields of interest, that of migration, that of minority group relations, and that of Latin American culture. We have tried, because of the nature of our data, to join psychological interviews with demographic facts on migration; the Puerto Ricans are the first sizable group from outside the continent to enter a large United States city since the immigration laws of the twenties, and as such have caused us to reconsider to some extent the problems of migration. As for minority group problems, the Puerto Rican story is of interest in that many of the migrants are of mixed race, and thus at once Negro and foreign. At the same time they are of Latin American culture, which allows us to present a close-up of certain features of this culture in contact with North American traits.

2

METhod

Our account is based upon a study begun in September, 1947, which has involved some nine major phases: (1) In planning the work, we gathered such documentary facts and figures as were available and interviewed various officials of the Puerto Rican government in San Juan, New York, and Washington, D.C., as well as state and city officials in New York and heads of various welfare and social agencies in New York City. We also held interviews and conferences with people in less formal contact with the New York migrants. (2) Soon, into the New York colonies we began to send Puerto Rican observers who participated in the life of the migrants, writing memoranda from their experiences, and recording intensive interviews. These interviews were open-ended, and often recorded only after leaving the informant. The resulting materials were used to draw up a design for the more extensive field work to be launched. (3) In the meantime, we had begun the design of an area sample and of an objective interview guide which could profitably be used on a larger scale and by less experienced interviewers. This structured guide was the result of a "translation" of the problems and findings of the informal field work of phase two into an instrument of workable questions. (4) The guide was pretested by members of our intensive interview staff, as well as by people we were training for the larger field work; after approximately one hundred interviews (not used in the final data) and some half dozen revisions of the draft as a whole, the guide was ready for use with a sample of the migrants. (5) Between January and May, 1948, we worked in Spanish Harlem and Morrisania, completing 1113 interviews, located within our area sample of households, each requiring from 45 minutes to 2½ hours to complete. In these interviews with one member of each of the 1113 households, we also obtained a few objective facts about all other household members, thus allowing us to expand our information on these points to cover some 5000 Puerto Ricans in the city. (6) We began this field work with some sixty-five interviewers, most of them Puerto Ricans, a few from Latin American countries. During the first ten days of field work, this number was cut to thirty interviewers, who were checked daily for sample instructions and whose interviews were gone over in detail with the field supervisors. (7) As the interviews began to come in satisfactorily, we constructed an appropriate code and began to train a coding staff, using in so far as we could our more talented interviewers who were familiar with the guide and its operation in the field. Four Hollerith cards for each respondent and one "household" card for each of the 5000 people on whom we had census type information were punched. (8) A preliminary statistical draft of the extensive interview materials was prepared; this presented the straight-run answers to each question used and a few simple cross tabulations. (9) After a pause during the summer, we began in the fall of 1948 an over-all analysis of our documents, intensive interviews, participant observations, and statistical data. This analysis has resulted in the present report.

3

In a study of this sort, the authors are of course indebted to many persons and institutions. Foremost among these is the Puerto Rican government which financed the work, and its officials, especially Mr. Fernando Sierra Berdecia, Commissioner of Labor, who gave our various reports and administrative suggestions serious consideration but who, after accepting our design, allowed us a completely free hand to do the work as we saw fit, and to write it as we felt it should be written. We also benefited from suggestions from staff members of the Welfare Council of New York City, local and state departments of public welfare, the Community Service Society, and the New York School of Social Work.

Ninety-five per cent of the Puerto Rican migrants whom our interviewers approached welcomed the interviewers and devoted their time to being questioned, often on personal and family matters; we thank them, as well as our interviewers who for several months walked streets and climbed stairs, patiently counting dwelling units and conducting interviews.

The office and field staff included Miss Ann Lohmann, who was a prime mover of much of the field work, kept a sharp eye on the sample from day to day, and was in charge of gathering documentary materials for its design; Miss Monserat Zayas, who supervised the coding and later assisted in the processing of the statistical data; Mrs. Ruth Senior, who supervised field work and the coding as well as assisting in an earlier statistical draft of the materials; Miss Elena Padilla, Mr. Charles Rosario, Miss Carmen Isales, and Mr. Robert Lawrence, whose intensive interviews and close-up memoranda from the field were indispensable to the design and execution of the work; Mrs. Ruth Harper Mills, who was in charge of the statistical analysis presented in the chapter on adaptation and offered many suggestions on the statistics and the editing of the entire volume; Mr. William Wachs, whose consultation did much to simplify and improve the translation of the final interview guide into Spanish; and Miss Beatrice Kevitt, who greatly improved the readability of the manuscript by her editorial skill and diligence.

Rose Kohn Goldsen as Assistant Director and Senior Analyst, was in charge of the statistical analysis, from the coding to the final phase; she contributed many of the ideas contained in the study. Clarence Senior, who joined the staff as Associate Director in January, 1948, brought to the work his knowledge of Puerto

Rico and of migration; he was primarily responsible for documentary materials, and trained and directed the interviewers for the extensive phase of the field work in New York. C. Wright Mills, as Director of the study, designed it, was in charge of its execution, and is the senior author of the present volume. The authors consider the work a joint endeavor and share responsibility for any deficiencies it may contain.

ONE:

THE ISLAND

"We are in a strange country."

—*From an interview
with a Puerto Rican
migrant.*

1. *The Island*

IF THE United States were as crowded as Puerto Rico, it would contain almost all the people of the world. This Caribbean island, 35 miles wide, 100 miles long, now holds slightly more than two million people, more than twice the number fifty years ago. Since 1898, when Spain ceded Puerto Rico to the United States, many changes as startling as that in population have beset the traditional pattern of Puerto Rican life. As one observer writes, "More happened in the first two decades of American life than in the four centuries of Spanish occupation."[1]

Yet American influences have by no means replaced the strongly Latin cultural climate of the island. Spanish Puerto Rico was preindustrial and predemocratic; American ideas of democracy and the practices of modern industrial society are directly antithetical to the four-hundred-year-old Spanish heritage of tyranny and an agricultural, patriarchal, static society. Politically reinforcing the tensions between the two cultures, United States rule has been profoundly ambiguous, its policy in some matters that of the old-style imperialistic state, in others that of the modern democracy. Puerto Ricans have been United States citizens since 1917, but until 1948 did not elect their own governor; they elect a voting representative to national party conventions, but do not vote for the President of the United States, nor are they represented in Congress by voting members. The incoherent political position of the Puerto Ricans symbolizes the discontinuity of their total situation. While most cultures are mixtures of several elements, as is certainly that of the United States, Puerto Rican culture is peculiarly bifurcated, each ele-

3

ment pointing to an alternate way of life, neither of which is quite adequate to present conditions in Puerto Rico.

I

When Spain settled Puerto Rico in the beginning of the sixteenth century, the tribal structure of the aboriginal Boriquen Indians, a primitive agricultural group, was destroyed, and replaced only by Spanish overlordship and mercantilist exploitation. For centuries the people were ruled by feudal landlords, exploited by Spanish merchants, and denied civil rights. There was frequent and arbitrary censorship and seizure of local newspapers. Before 1898, 83 per cent of the people were illiterate; 92 per cent of the children were not in school; the island's death rate ranged between 25 and 35 per 1000; sanitary and health facilities were virtually absent.[2]

Dissatisfaction with Spanish colonial policy had long been expressed by secret societies which organized boycotts against Spaniards in business, and attempted to educate Puerto Rican children in spite of the official hostility to schooling. During the nineteenth century small bourgeois elements led the fight against Spanish political rule, and there were at least three sizeable insurrections. The widening rift with Spain, in the years before American occupation, had also been economic. Between 1893 and 1896 the United States supplied 24 per cent of all imports to Puerto Rico, Spain providing 32 per cent.[3] Although some of the Puerto Ricans who welcomed the United States soldier in 1898 hoped that the island would be given its independence, others, for business or ideological reasons, wanted a permanent tie to the fast-expanding economy of the world's largest formal democracy.

However rapid the change to United States rule may have been politically and economically, in language, religion, and many other aspects, Puerto Rico retains its character as a Spanish colony. Even today the Puerto Rican carries on his everyday activities in Spanish—in reading the newspaper, talking to friends, doing business. The mixing of races has been going on since the beginning of the sixteenth century, and the variety of racial types is similar to that of other former Spanish colonies, ranging from blue-eyed, blond Caucasians to dark-skinned Negroes. At first only Spanish men migrated to Puerto Rico, and the children of their unions with Indian women, the mestizos, were numerous. Ever since Negroes were introduced as slaves in 1529, whites, Indians, mestizos, and Negroes have interbred. By 1777, the Indians, as a pure race, were almost extinct.[4] In a single family, some members may be classified as "white," others as "colored." However, the proportion classed as "Negro" by the United States Census has decreased steadily since 1899, when it was 38.2 per cent, until in 1940 it was 23.5 per cent.[5]

In Puerto Rico, as in all Spanish colonies, the Catholic church was established as a state institution. By the end of the nineteenth century Catholicism in Puerto Rico became relaxed and indulgent, but the Catholic church, with all the sanction available to an official religion, continued to control the spiritual and moral life of the islanders.

When the island became a United States territory, the Catholic church was disestablished. For the first time, Protestant missionaries were allowed to work on the island. They built schools and trained teachers to carry on the missions, and began to secure converts; at present about 15 per cent of the population are Protestant. The bulk of the population continues to be formally Catholic, but many are not strict in their practice. Of the 94 per cent of one sample (interviewed in the tobacco, coffee, and fruit areas) who were formally Catholic, only 62 per cent attended church somewhat regularly. In the sugar cane region, 96.5 per cent were Catholics, but only 57 per cent of these attended church. Church attendance among Protestants, however, was 81.3 and 68.5 per cent respectively in the two regions.[6] At many points, where American ideas conflict with Catholic doctrine, many Puerto Ricans accept the former as part of the new turn of events.

Spiritualistic groups have secured some followers, although not as many as any formal religion. The Spiritualists usually deny that they are practicing religion or that their meeting places are churches, but their beliefs seem to be spreading. Protestant or Catholic church members often attend seances and participate in spiritualistic activities; spiritualistic remedies may be used in case of illness, and the curandero, the medicine man, distributes charms and herbs in many villages.

2

There is no unilateral status hierarchy in Puerto Rico. Part of the essential meaning of her cultural conflicts is that the ways of securing status have become confused, with consequent loss of the internal security which status brought in the old established society. Superimposed on the older Spanish patterns based on birth and family is the newer American model, heavily weighted by economic class. Those with high status origin and high income are undoubtedly at the top; those with low status origin and low income, at the bottom; but those with low origin but with high income are overtaking those with high origin but without high income. That is the historical trend; in general, the plain facts of economic class lead more surely to high prestige than the traditional prestige of higher family circles. However, interesting coincidences develop between the two competing status systems: both look down on the Negro worker, the Spanish because he is a worker; the American, because he is a Negro.

Throughout Puerto Rican society there runs this conflict of status ideal and mannerism. Proud of the island's connection with Spain, educated Puerto Ricans point to that country's rich past: the paintings of El Greco and Goya; the literature of Cervantes and Lope de Vega. Argentine and Mexican movies bring the customs and characters, the costumes and clichés of the current Spanish world to the Puerto Rican screen. The Spanish-oriented section of the upper class displays wrought-iron gates and fences and mudéjar tiles. Yet this conscious orientation to Spanish tradition is mainly confined to certain sections of the upper classes, having more to do with the status sphere of Puerto Rican society than with the economic or political order.

Although the Puerto Rican grows up in a proud identification with Spanish culture, he identifies himself at the same time with the United States. Economically and politically the island is not "Spanish"; it is under the influence and even the domination of the United States, whose influence is not only political and economic. The Puerto Rican's tastes are modified by mainland advertising; his language is full of English words and phrases. His public values are bound up with American democratic teachings, however bitter he might feel about the gap between United States principles and United States practice on the island.

The Puerto Rican has also, in some part, adopted American patterns of race consciousness. He either feels inferior because he is too dark and therefore can be looked down upon; more secure because he is light-skinned; or, if he is one of the several intermediate types, he acquires something of the American ambivalence. Those Puerto Ricans who can prove they are pure white often make a point of doing so.[7]

When the Spaniards, who are Caucasians, represented authority on the island, the colonial, in his aspiration to achieve equality with his rulers, began to adopt their attitudes toward race. Thus, even before 1898, while the Negro was not discriminated against, the Caucasian had higher status, and wherever it was possible to do so, Negro blood was denied. But the Spaniard's racial intolerance was more subtle than the rigid distinction made in the United States, and despite the growing infiltration of United States standards, the colored Puerto Rican does possess a feeling of racial security in his own environment. Everyone is first a Puerto Rican and only second a member of a particular racial group. Problems concerning race are status problems for each individual rather than genuine "racial" problems. The Puerto Rican, generally, makes racial classifications on the basis of skin color and physical appearance, rather than actual or imputed racial heritage. Any person who is light enough, and who has "good hair," is usually considered, and considers himself, white. However, upper-class groups who pride themselves on their "whiteness" pay careful attention to family name and can identify individuals who have colored ancestors, even though these people appear to be white and are accepted as white in some circles. Except in the "best" families, discrimination is only subtly apparent in social affairs, and is unlikely to occur in other spheres of life—in employment opportunities or business contacts.

3

Kinship, which is the social hub of Puerto Rican society, is still organized in the Spanish tradition. Ostensible power in the family resides in the male, although women are responsible for the daily routine. There are exceptions. In some families, relationships are based on a more balanced give-and-take; in others, the father may be uninterested in his prerogatives, or may even be dominated by his wife. Compared with continental, American family types, however, the despotic father-husband relationship is the dominant island pattern.

Another Latin heritage in Puerto Rican family structure is the extension of the primary family group to include an extended clan of relatives. The family unit frequently includes not only the father, mother, and their children, but also aunts and uncles, cousins and grandparents, nieces and nephews. It sometimes includes the couple who sponsor one of the children, the "compadre" and "comadre" (literally co-father and co-mother). If a child is deprived of the care of his parents by death or illness or is abandoned by them, a relative usually takes over. Relatives help each other as a duty because they all are "of the same blood"; a mother trusts the care of her child to relatives without misgivings. The Puerto Rican recognizes other family obligations and duties which may seem strange to continentals. Old people are given tremendous respect; ritual kin are taken seriously; children contribute such money as they earn to the family pool. A sort of feudal attitude still obtains towards servants, who are considered household members for whom the family is responsible. This extended family is politically relevant, for nepotism is often expected and is conventionally approved.

In the Latin family it is customary for the boys to have a great deal of personal freedom, but for the girls to be carefully supervised. In the middle- and upper-class families girls are protected by chaperonage, except in the more sophisticated environment of the capital. Until a girl has become formally engaged, she is permitted to have only supervised contact with nonfamily men. In lower-class families this supervision is rare; these girls marry young, often in a common-law (consensual) marriage without a civil or religious ceremony.

The male is supposed to be dominant, proof of his manhood being in direct relation to his sexual capacity. The woman is supposed to be submissive, and her submissiveness is guaranteed by a network of manners and politenesses which confines her major sphere of activities to the home, circumscribes her social contacts, and places her under constant surveillance. As an incidental consequence, she is likely to overprotect her children.

To the outside observer, the Puerto Rican pattern for women seems divided into two extreme types; either she seems to be dominated and repressed first by her family, later by her husband; or she seems to have apparent sexual freedom in an informal marriage relationship. Actually each pattern contains elements of the other: the supervised girl or wife has often managed to secure for herself much more psychological and physical freedom than is apparent; the seemingly unsupervised lower-class woman is frequently much more restricted and dominated than appearances might indicate.

The number of illegitimate births in Puerto Rico, compared with the mainland, is relatively high. In 1946 the island's illegitimacy rate was 33.7 per cent, the rate being higher in rural than in urban areas.[8] An anthropological study of a town in southwestern Puerto Rico in 1946 found consensual marriages among about 50 per cent of the nonskilled people; only about 25 per cent of the skilled workers, and none of the business and professional group were consensually married.[9] The 1940 census reported 26.4 per cent of all married women in consensual relation, the rural rate being slightly higher than the urban.[10]

The economic factor may have much to do with acceptance of common-law union. Especially in the isolated rural communities, a church marriage is very expensive, since it involves a marriage fee, a trip into town, a ceremony which requires at least a bridal gown in white—the symbol of the virgin—as well as the costly incidentals which usually accompany celebrations in Spanish countries. It is less trouble for many people simply to live together, and common-law marriages may be as stable as legal ones.

In the city, slum poverty prompts common-law marriages and also provides the disorganization which entails unstable relationships. In general, however, a woman who has had two or three husbands in succession does not consider herself promiscuous. She has been faithful to each man in his turn, and has borne children to each of them, the support of whom the next husband accepts as part of the necessary inconveniences of married life. Psychiatric workers believe that many of the emotional difficulties of these children can be traced to tensions and neglect in homes where the children of former unions are rejected.

4

Throughout its history, Puerto Rico's educational institutions have been under the control of political and cultural outsiders, first Spanish, then American. There was no locally responsible commissioner of education until 1949. As the base of education in Puerto Rico has been enlarging, it has shifted from its tie-in with the old status system to the new economy and its apparent political needs. The Spanish emphasis upon the liberal arts was a part of the leisurely upper-class style of life; since the middle thirties it has been supplemented, and now seems to be overtaken, by vocational routines under the industrial aspiration. Education and the certified titles it confers are more highly regarded in Puerto Rico than in most United States communities, somewhat as political careers there bring greater status.

Puerto Rico's educational level is much lower than the continent's. In 1940 about one third of the Puerto Rican population

(31.5 per cent) could neither read nor write (San Juan, 17 per cent), compared with the mainland's negligible illiteracy rate. Average yearly expenditure per Puerto Rican school child in 1943-4 was $40.58, compared with the mainland average of $117.36 (Mississippi, $42.35; New York State, $198.49).[11] Yet some 40 per cent of those from 5 to 20 years of age were, in 1940, attending school on the island, compared with the mainland figure of 52.6 per cent (and Mississippi's 50.9 per cent). Moreover, whatever primary education the Puerto Rican does receive is of a poorer caliber than the equivalent schooling available to the mainlander.

Rural districts are even further behind than urban. On the island as a whole, slightly less than half of all children of school age attend school; but in the city, 80 per cent attend school, in the country, 40 per cent. Half of all children, rural and urban, who do enroll in the first grade drop out before they reach the sixth. In the 1006 one-room rural schools, the student load per teacher is around 60.[12]

All the contradictions between English- and Spanish-speaking culture are carried into the classroom. That the islanders use Spanish rather than English has been a continual source of difficulty between the mainland and the island. As a major key to the acceptance of new cultural patterns, the Puerto Rican educational system was designed by continentals who, in an effort to facilitate that acceptance, immediately introduced English into the schools of the new possession.

The attempt to teach even the "tool" subjects—reading, writing, and arithmetic—in English went on for some forty years, the mother tongue, Spanish, being relegated to the place of a subject. This was done in spite of the obvious fact that the school population, like the population at large, knew no English, and in the face of the all but unanimous stand against such a policy by many continental and insular educators as well as popular dissatisfaction in Puerto Rico. The older people—who were children before 1898—have learned English only as it was necessary or convenient. In many households, the parents know no English at all. Even if the Puerto Rican does know English, he generally has a much better command of it for reading and writing than for conversation.

Moreover the teachers sent to the island were very poorly trained; some knew no Spanish. Indeed, the continental educator's ignorance of Puerto Rico and its people went so far that insular teachers, assumed to be Indians, were trained at Carlisle or Haskel Indian institutes!

Such an irresponsible policy of educating the islanders has resulted in incalculable harm. According to Dr. Mariano Villaronga, Commissioner of Education in 1949, "The results of this practice are the obvious ones of lack of progress in both English and in the subject taught; a tendency to memorize by rote without understanding; discouragement with the whole learning process; and a prejudice against English as the cause of the whole trouble."[13] The Puerto Rican often characterizes the situation with the phrase, "We are illiterate in two languages!"

American educational measures, as regards language at least, have only brought confusion over the goals to be attained, with the result that the advantages of knowing English as a cultural and business asset are denied, overlooked, or overemphasized in the struggle between linguistic tendencies.

Yet, in spite of all the handicaps and mistakes, the island's educational level has risen substantially and is continuing to do so. Now, only one third of the population can neither read nor write. In 1899 three fourths were illiterate. While only half the children of school age are now in school, in 1900 the percentage was only 10.5. The yearly expenditure for education per child is $40.58, but in 1910 the amount was $11.29. Moreover, the task in Puerto Rico is not small; 40.7 per cent of the Puerto Ricans are of school age.[14]

The islanders do very much want schooling for their children. Under the influence of cooperatives and labor unions, and a broad-scale government program, the budget for public education has increased rapidly. In 1941 it was $6,000,000; in 1948, $36,-221,000.[15] The desire for higher education is also reflected in the increase in enrollment at the University of Puerto Rico, a growth of over 1000 per cent in the twenty-three years following 1925–26, from 897 to 10,000 students.[16]

Spanish standards of gentleman's work still do somewhat affect educational aims. Many children are raised to be proud of their inability to work with their hands and to disdain manual work. But such attitudes are waning, and vocational education is reaching more and more people. A rural junior high school program is being developed, and eleven regional vocational education schools are being built to supplement the University's School of Industrial Arts.

5

The various institutions of the Puerto Rican social structure have never been articulated into institutional orders as autonomous as those in non-Spanish western countries. Since the advent of United States rule, Puerto Rico's economy has been based on the new kind of mercantilism which has been developing in the twentieth century. With no intermediate period of laissez-faire ideas and economy, Puerto Rico has entered the new political economy directly from a preindustrial kind of colonialism. Thus the economic order, as well as every other part of the Puerto Rican social structure, has been and is now subordinated to the political order. Today, the political relation of Puerto Rico to the United States is a controlling fact of the society.

As a colony of the United States, on which it is dependent economically and militarily, it is in the anomalous position of being one of the few territories owned by the democratic United States, and is subject to the vagaries of the shifting policies of changing national administrations. Soon after the United States took over from autocratic Spain, the insular government was controlled by the sugar companies and the old ruling class, who looked to Washington without much fear.

American governmental machinery has not lent itself to the successful government of a colony. Until 1934 the island was under the jurisdiction of the War Department, at which time it was transferred to the Department of the Interior. The island's affairs are subject to the decisions of federal employees more than a thousand miles across the ocean, few of whom are acquainted with the problems at first hand, and only a handful of whom spend their full time on insular affairs. These government officials who ordinarily deal with programs involving 148 million people on the continent have difficulty adjusting their thoughts to the different needs of 2 million islanders.

In Congress, Puerto Rico has a nonvoting representative, but continental legislators who may have no knowledge and frequently no interest in the island—whose first responsibility is to their voting constituents—sit on the committees that deal with Puerto Rican problems.[17] National policies are, in some cases, applied whether or not they fit the local circumstances. Sometimes United States policy seems to reveal procrastination of great length: for example, the crucial post of Commissioner of Education was vacant from 1945 to January, 1949. The commissioner was one of the insular officials appointed by the President of the United States "with the advice and consent of the Senate." Two presidential nominees were unable to get over the hurdle of senatorial confirmation. The newly elected governor has been given the power to appoint the commissioner. Insular finances have always been subsidized by the federal government, and federal taxes paid in Puerto Rico are earmarked for Puerto Rican expenditures. Insular citizens pay no federal income tax.

The island has a measure of political autonomy, but it is not self-governing. As was pointed out earlier, island Puerto Ricans have no voting representatives in Congress, nor can they vote in presidential elections. Not until 1948 did they elect their own governor; he had always been appointed by the President of the United States.[18] The Puerto Rican legislature, which is popularly elected, has jurisdiction over many local affairs, but laws passed by it may be vetoed by the President or by Congress. With such a safety valve, though it has rarely been used, insular legislators can seldom feel a final responsibility for their acts. The very enlargement of the areas of autonomous decision has led to further tensions; untried ways have had to be integrated into political life and personality, and new power has brought new and unaccustomed responsibilities, both political and non-political.

The concessions to democracy which the United States has made are, according to the Chancellor of the University of Puerto Rico, "obviously insufficient, much less than what is due both to Puerto Rico and the United States."[19] The islanders feel keenly the disparity between United States democratic principles and the practice regarding Puerto Rico. For the past several years the island legislature has unanimously petitioned Congress to allow their people to vote on the alternatives of statehood, independence, or a "dominion" form of government. Uncertainty about possible future changes in the political status of the island is a handicap to economic advancement. Dissatisfaction with the island's ambiguous political status is a source of bitter feeling towards the United States among many Puerto Ricans, especially the Independentistas.

Yet, in spite of all this political uncertainty, within its present framework Puerto Rico has made significant social improvements. But the most crucial problem, that of increasing productivity to support the crowded and growing population, remains. For almost a decade the Puerto Rican government has been working toward this end.

The war interfered in many crucial ways, but the war also gave the government more income with which to work. The increase in rum consumption on the continent raised governmental income well above previous years (the insular budget receives the proceeds of the federal internal revenue tax on rum). Attempts are being made to democratize land ownership, diversify and improve agriculture, attract new industries and develop those in which private investors are not interested, to raise wages and labor productivity, provide pure water, insure against industrial accidents and illness and coffee crop damage, clear slums, build low-cost housing, improve labor relations, increase electricity generation and distribution, modernize the transportation and communication systems, provide wholesome public recreation, raise the quality of tobacco produced, open dry sections of the island to farming by irrigation, improve public administration, and, on the basis of research, plan for the future.[20]

6

When the United States took over the island in 1898, Puerto Rico's main crops were coffee and tobacco. Whether or not the island could have continued to support itself by concentrating on these crops is debatable. At any rate, under United States protection, sugar—a cash crop, largely plantation grown—has become the dominant factor in the economy.

The sugar industry depends upon the tariff, a political arrangement which is fixed not on the island but in the United States. The quotas for the amount of sugar to be raised and the amount to be refined on the island (set at insular levels of consumption) are decided politically and from the outside. Puerto Rico, a rural society which must import food, is economically dependent upon the export of raw materials, semiprocessed, and hand-manufactured goods. Its economy is even more a political economy than that of midcentury America.

From 1899 to 1939 sugar cane acreage was increased 400 per cent.[21] In 1948, 52 per cent of all agricultural workers (20 per cent of all the gainfully employed) were working on sugar lands.[22] In the years just before the war, sugar and its derivatives provided about 65 per cent of the island's exports.[23] Industries not connected with sugar have, by comparison, expanded only slightly. As more and more lands have been turned over to sugar, the sugar economy has penetrated into almost every sphere of life on the island.

The preamble to the Land Law of 1941 summarizes the fact of sugar domination: "The sugar latifundia has spread its tentacles within the vast area of its dominions, to the operation of commercial and industrial establishments, and of grocery and general stores; has limited the circulation of money, has caused the annihilation of communal life in many of the urban centers; has made it impossible for thousands of human beings to be the owners of even the lot where their homes are situated, all to the consequent unbalancing of the economic structure of the Island and to the grave endangering of the peace, the tranquility, the dignity, and the economic and social freedom of the people of Puerto Rico."[24]

But there is another side to the picture. In order to maintain its large population, Puerto Rico must utilize its resources to support the greatest possible number of workers and to return the greatest cash income. There is not enough land—certainly not enough rich land—to permit a fully diversified agriculture. If the island is to remain agricultural, a cash crop such as sugar is a source of greater income and greater employment.

Yet, this very concentration on sugar growing forces the island into an economic squeeze. Land ownership is concentrated in huge estates; cane workers are seasonally unemployed; since so much of the available land is devoted to sugar, the island must import about half its foodstuffs at high costs. Most important, much of the sugar land has been exhausted, so that the cost of growing cane in Puerto Rico is much greater than in other areas. Were it not for United States tariff protection, Puerto Rican sugar would be unable to compete with sugar from other West Indian areas, such as Cuba or the Dominican Republic.

The Puerto Rican government is attempting to meet the problems created by the sugar latifundia in two ways. First, through the Land Authority, it is attempting to democratize land ownership and to improve and diversify agriculture. One of the purposes of this program is to help keep the farmer on the land. Some 15,000 families had been settled on small plots of from ¼ to 3 acres by July, 1947. There they could supplement their incomes by growing vegetables for home consumption or local trade. Cooperative organization helps stretch cash income in the 139 colonies thus far formed.[25] Secondly, the government is attempting to encourage industrialization on the island. Even though Puerto Rico is still largely agricultural, there has been an unmistakable shift in sources of employment.

TABLE I-1.   SOURCES OF EMPLOYMENT IN PUERTO RICO, 1910 AND 1947[26]

Industry group	1910	1947
Agriculture	61%	39%
Manufacturing and construction	13	24
Trade and transportation	10	17
Services (incl. government)	16	20
TOTAL CIVILIAN EMPLOYMENT	100%	100%

The proportion of the island's labor force working in agriculture has declined considerably since 1910; many people find jobs in the island's manufacturing and construction industries, trade and transportation, and services.

The gainfully employed increased 64 per cent in the 38 years from 1910 to 1947, 51 per cent of this rise occurring in the last 7 years.[27] During the war and the immediate postwar period, the income of the Puerto Rican people reached its historical peak, although it is still relatively low by United States standards. Per capita net income rose from $121 in 1939–40 to $239 in 1943–44. Preliminary estimates indicate that the 1945–46 per capita reached $262, and that it fell to $256 the following year.[28]

As a sugar-producing area, Puerto Rico shares the economic fate of plantation economies: her people are poor, undernourished, and landless. Some 39 per cent of the islanders were still employed in agriculture in 1947. Their weekly earnings during March, 1945, averaged $5.00; in manufacturing, $12. In the same period, weekly earnings in manufacturing in the United States were $47.50, yet prices on the island are approximately the same as they are in New York City.[29] Obviously, the "average" Puerto Rican has great difficulty making ends meet.

Judged by North American standards of life, Puerto Rico's 2 million are frightfully poor; by Latin American standards, however, the Puerto Ricans are quite well off. In the middle forties, the level of living on the island was low compared with the poorer states in the Union, but higher than in other Caribbean islands. In terms of per capita income measured in dollars, Puerto Rico is ahead of most Latin American Republics.[30] This economic situation is symbolic of Puerto Rico's intermediate position between North and South in the western hemisphere.

7

Puerto Rico has few rivals and no equals in rate of population increase. In the past half century the difference between the death and birth rates—the rate of natural increase—has more than doubled,[31] and as a result the population has more than doubled since the American occupation.

Actually this growth is chiefly due to a decline of more than 50 per cent in the death rate, rather than to an increased birth rate. Sanitary and health conditions under Spanish rule were so bad that a vigorous public health policy by the United States has been highly effective. Public health and sanitation measures have eliminated the smallpox and yellow fever that were endemic on the island fifty years ago. In the first year of United States occupation, the entire population was vaccinated; deaths from smallpox had averaged 621 annually in the previous nine years, but in the following ten months there was only one.[32] Infant mortality, although still high, was reduced from 138.4 per thousand live births in 1937 to 71.5 in 1947 and 67.6 in 1949.[33]

However, the average Puerto Rican is still less well fed than the average mainlander, he is still more susceptible to diseases, and his life expectation is 8 to 20 years less.[34] Infant diseases, as well as tuberculosis, pneumonia, and many other causes of death, are directly related to low incomes. In cities, the proportion of still births is five times as great among those in the "less than $200" income class as in the "$3000 and over" class.[35] The shorter stature and lighter weight sometimes thought characteristic of the Puerto Ricans is also to a large extent a class phenomenon. Groups better off economically are taller, heavier, and generally healthier than most peasants and workers.[36]

The death rate is susceptible to further decreases, as levels of living are raised and public health work increases in scope and in effectiveness.[37] But probably the population growth will continue for some time in any case, even though Puerto Rico is one of the most overcrowded places in the world. The island's population is relatively young, and therefore there is a high proportion of persons of child-bearing age.

Acute disbalance of population and resources creates downward pressure on levels of living which demands some safety valve. Resources can be increased or made more productive; population, or at least rate of increase, can be reduced. Since land as a resource is automatically limited, it must be used to the limit of its productivity. Industrialization is another possible technique; an industrial area can support greater numbers than an agricultural one. As noted, Puerto Rico has recently embarked upon a rather large-scale industrialization program.[38] Yet despite this, as the birthrate continues high, and the death rate declines, the pressure on levels of living continues.

There remain but two civilized recourses: to control the number of births, or to encourage substantial migration from the island.[39]

A Puerto Rican of the present generation, therefore, finds himself caught in a situation which strongly encourages him to leave the island. His Spanish cultural ties might be expected to draw him to the Latin American countries. But he is not a Latin American; he has soaked up continental United States culture —from a distance of 1000 miles; he has become a Puerto Rican American. If he is to leave the island, his standard of living, his way of life, his mannerisms, his values make the pull of the States especially strong. These general cultural and specific economic pulls, along with the unrestricted migration which the Puerto Rican enjoys as a citizen of the United States, have operated so that migration from Puerto Rico has meant, by and large, migration to the United States mainland.

Consequently, Puerto Rico is at present undergoing considerable population movement.[40] There is internal migration, from city to city, and from country to city; there is a good deal of overseas movement; from the island to the mainland, principally to New York City. The population pressures upon the island are so acute and the need for adjustment so grave that these movements can be expected to continue.

2.   *The Migrants*

Some 200,000 Puerto Rican Americans lived in New York City in 1948.[1] Stretching from 100th to 125th Street, from Third to Fifth Avenue, in Spanish Harlem, are the densest clusters of Puerto Ricans, 50 to 75 per cent in most of the blocks. In the 80-some blocks of the Morrisania section of the lower east side of the Bronx, between 25 to 50 per cent of the approximately 20,000 households are Puerto Rican. There are other pockets of Puerto Rican settlement in the city: in the lower east side near the Bowery; in the Chelsea district; at several points along Second Avenue. But the blocks in Spanish Harlem and Morrisania constitute the core areas of Puerto Rican settlement in New York.

During the early years of this century, Puerto Rican cigar-makers settled on the lower east side. They were followed by merchant seamen on the island-to-New York run, who congregated near the Brooklyn waterfront, and by women garment workers who were brought to sew in local factories. Since then, increasing numbers of islanders have been finding their way to the metropolis. Until about a year ago, Brooklyn constituted another major core area of Puerto Rican settlement, but the dwellings in that area were torn down, dispersing the Puerto Rican families who had been living there through the borough.

The migrant who follows the general migration pattern will, upon his arrival, gravitate to one or the other of the present core areas. Here he finds relatives or former townsmen who help him find living quarters and a job, and in general ease him through his first contact with his new home. After a time, the migrant who becomes acclimated to the city—especially if he has been economically successful—may move out of these areas of first settlement. He loses his former identity in non-Puerto Rican neighborhoods in Inwood, Queens, Long Island, Jersey, and usually, at best, maintains but minimal contact with the old areas of first settlement. That is, if he is white. But if he is a Negro, because his residential mobility is much more limited, he is forced to stay where he is.

The aim of the present study has *not* been to track down and survey all Puerto Ricans who have made the journey from the island to the city. Such a study would have required a complete census of a scope far beyond the means available to us. We are describing only those Puerto Rican migrants who cluster geographically in the two major areas, Spanish Harlem and Morrisania.*

One fourth of the migrants now residing in Spanish Harlem and Morrisania have come since the end of the last war; about 19 per cent came during the war years; but more than half made the journey from the island to the city in the interwar period of the twenties and thirties.

TABLE II-1. PROPORTION OF PUERTO RICAN MIGRANTS ARRIVING IN SPANISH HARLEM AND MORRISANIA, TO 1948

Time of Arrival	Men	Women	All migrants
Postwar years (1946 to spring, 1948)	27%	24%	26%
War years (1942 to 1945)	20	19	19
Interwar years (1920 to 1941)	48	55	52
1919 or earlier	5	2	3
TOTAL (100%)	(417)	(696)	(1113)

* Since more whites than Negroes leave these centers, our study undoubtedly includes more colored migrants than their quota among all islanders in New York. By the same token, since the recent arrivals tend to gravitate first to these areas, our sample may include a greater proportion of those who have come to New York since 1940, and a correspondingly smaller proportion of those who came before that time.

The slight difference in the time of arrival of men and women (57 per cent of the women came before 1942 compared with 53 per cent of the men) may be a reflection of the fact that during the war years, while migration as a whole was restricted, certain numbers of men were brought to the mainland for war and industrial purposes.

The flow of migrants, the numbers entering the city each year, has increased considerably in recent years.

TABLE II-2.   ANNUAL RATE OF PUERTO RICAN
MIGRATION TO SPANISH HARLEM AND
MORRISANIA

Rate of entry for each year reported	Index (1920–29 = 100)
1947	448
1946	515
1945	314
1942–44	145
1940–41	130
1935–39	94
1930–34	64
1920–29	100

During the depression decade, 1930–1939, the migration stream receded below the level of the twenties: since then, it has risen sharply until 1946, the peak year of entry, when there were more than five times as many migrants as in any year in the twenties. In 1947, although the entrance rate was still well above that recorded in any year before World War II, it fell below 1946.

What kinds of people are those Puerto Ricans who have left the island during the past generation? There is widespread discussion in Puerto Rico about the characteristics of the migrants and speculations as to whether they are "average" islanders, or in some way out of the ordinary. How do they compare in age, sex, and race with those who do not leave? How do they compare in education, occupation, and skill? Has the character of the migration stream changed in any way during the past decades? If so, how do recent migrants differ from earlier ones? The attitude of both governmental and private bodies toward emigration as part of the solution to Puerto Rico's overpopulation depends somewhat upon the answers, and these answers indicate the kind of selection which has screened the migrants to New York's core settlements.

Almost every Puerto Rican type is represented in the migration, but each is represented to a greater or to a lesser degree. The question must be put in terms of a comparison between those who come and those who stay. In several aspects on which we have information, the Puerto Ricans who migrate to New York are not typical of the island's total population: (1) This migration contains a greater proportion of women than the island population; (2) nonwhites are represented in it in a slightly higher proportion; (3) the migrant colonists are somewhat older than the island's general population, because there are fewer children among them; but they include a greater proportion of people in productive age groups and a smaller proportion of older people; (4) there are more legally married and more divorced but fewer single persons among the migrants in the New York colonies than among islanders; (5) there are more literate persons, more with higher education; (6) it is primarily a migration of urban dwellers, who, incidentally, are relatively more stable geographically than the island's population as a whole; (7) there are higher proportions of skilled and semi-skilled workers, and fewer agricultural workers among them, and on the island they had been employed more regularly and had received a slightly higher income than the Puerto Rican average.

I

The Puerto Rican migration to New York has for many years contained more women than men. On the island as a whole, according to the 1940 census, there were an equal number of both sexes (sex ratio 100). In the island's urban centers, the proportion of men is lower (83 men to every 100 women); but among the migrants entering Spanish Harlem and Morrisania, there is an even greater difference (63 males for every 100 females).[2]

This preponderance of women has been constant throughout the period of migration. From 1930 to 1941, for every 100 women who entered New York from the island, there were but 40 men. Even during the war years, when more men were coming from the island to do war work in New York, only 65 men entered for every 100 women.

Among the colored migrants, women outnumber the men to an even greater degree. In the twenties, for example, there was an almost equal proportion of white men and women migrants (sex ratio 90); but there were only 30 Negro men for every 100 Negro women in that period, and 50 intermediate men for every 100 intermediate women. This imbalance holds true in every period, except among Negroes migrating in the postwar years, during which time the ratio of men to women was higher for the Negroes than for the other two racial groups.[3]

The general trend has been for both men and women migrants to enter the city in increasing numbers; but the rate of entry for the men dropped during 1947. In fact, the decrease of the rate of entries for all Puerto Rican migrants since 1946 is largely accounted for by the slackening off of Negro and intermediate male entries, and to a lesser extent, of Negro women.[4]

2

The racial inheritance of the Puerto Ricans is Spanish, Negro, and Caribbean Indian. The range in skin color is from white to black, but the island population is now predominantly white. The 1940 Census reported 76.5 per cent white Puerto Ricans on the island, 73.5 per cent in the urban areas and 68.5 per cent in San Juan. (Persons of mixed blood were classified as non-white.)[5]

The Puerto Ricans in New York City's core areas are nearly representative of the island urban population, although there are somewhat fewer white Puerto Ricans in the Manhattan colony (57 per cent) than on the island. The Bronx color ratio (77 per cent white) is the same as the island.

Although the color ratio in New York's two core settlements is the same for males and females in Puerto Rico, there are 10 per cent more white men than white women.

TABLE II-3. RACIAL COMPOSITION OF ADULT MEN AND WOMEN PUERTO RICAN MIGRANTS IN NEW YORK CITY'S TWO CORE AREAS

Race	Male	Female	All migrants
White	70%	60%	64%
Intermediate[a]	14	17	16
Negro[b]	16	23	20
TOTAL[c] (100%)	(415)	(695)	(1110)

[a] This includes the group known in Puerto Rico as *indio* and *grifo*. The "indio" has a copper cast to his skin and may have prominent cheek bones; the "grifo" may be quite light complexioned, with blue or gray eyes, but have kinky hair (pelo malo), or have some other combination of racial features.
[b] This group includes Negroes and mulattos.
[c] Excludes 3 cases whose race is not known.

More white than colored Puerto Ricans have come to New York from the island, but since 1942 the *rate* of colored migration has increased more rapidly. Before that year, the rate of entry was approximately the same for both groups. Nineteen forty-six was the peak year of migration for all migrants to these two areas; in that year about four times as many white Puerto Ricans, but about eight times as many intermediates and Negroes, arrived in the city as in any year during the twenties.

Again, these rates do not describe the flow of all Puerto Ricans to the city. Since the bulk of our interviews were made in an area which Negroes do not leave, Negroes are represented relatively more strongly in the sample than whites.

3

The Puerto Rican migration conforms to the generally established fact that "voluntary migration is largely a phenomenon of youth."[6] The migrants are selected from the more productive age groups of the island population. Some 61 per cent of all the migrants during the forties were between the ages of 18 and 39.

The Puerto Ricans in New York have fewer children than stay-at-home islanders; therefore, they—including all the family members of the migrants interviewed—are older than the island community. The median age of the Puerto Rican population in Harlem and the Bronx is 24.2 years, which is nearly five years older than the median age of the islanders in 1940, but closely approximates the median age in San Juan. The men are slightly younger than the women. Even including the family members, the Puerto Ricans in New York, more than the islanders, tend to cluster in the productive age groups.

TABLE II-4. AGE OF PUERTO RICAN MIGRANTS AND THEIR FAMILIES
IN NEW YORK CITY'S TWO CORE AREAS OF SETTLEMENT
COMPARED WITH THE AGE OF ISLAND POPULATION (1940)

| Age | Migrants: 1947 | | | Puerto Rico:[a] |
	Male	Female	Total	1940
Under 9	23%	19%	21%	29%
10–19	21	20	20	23
20–29	19	22	21	19
30–39	17	17	17	11
40–49	13	12	12	8
50–59	5	6	6	5
60 and over	2	4	3	5
TOTAL (100%)	(2259)	(2661)	(4920)	(1,869,255)
MEDIAN	23.2	24.9	24.2	20.0

[a] Source: U. S. Census, 1940. Puerto Rico, *Population*, Bulletin 2, pp. 10–11.

Fewer members of the New York colonies are in the younger age groups (under 20 years old), and fewer are in the older age groups (50 and over) than is the case on the island. Thus, 50 per cent of the colonists, but only 38 per cent of the islanders, are from 20 to 49 years of age.

4

New York's Puerto Rican colonists are more likely to be legally married, less likely to be single or living together consensually than the islanders. The Puerto Rican colony also includes a greater proportion of divorced men and women than does the island population. Only 11 per cent of the migrants over 18 years of age are unmarried; almost two thirds are legally married; 8 per cent are divorced or widowed. Only 6 per cent reported a consensual marriage, which is less than half the percentage shown for Puerto Rico by the 1940 census.

The women in the Puerto Rican colonies are more likely than the men to be divorced, separated, or widowed. The colored migrants, both men and women, are more likely than the white to be consensually rather than legally married.[7]

TABLE II-5. PROPORTION OF DIVORCED AND SEPARATED MIGRANTS IN NEW YORK CITY'S CORE AREAS AND IN PUERTO RICO BY SEX

	Divorced and separated men	Divorced and separated women
Migrants	4.0%	16.0%
Islanders[a]	1.4%	6.4%

[a] Figures for Puerto Rico are from unpublished data from the WPA Survey of Incomes and Expenditures of Wage Earners 1941–42. These figures include persons 15 years old or over; the figures for the migrants include persons 18 years old or more.

Women migrants are two and a half times as likely to be divorced or separated as island women, men less likely than women to be divorced either in New York or on the island; but even so, the migrants include three times as large a share of divorced or separated males as are on the island.

The proportion of divorced women in the island's urban centers is available only from census data—and these figures report only legal divorces, not informal separations. Still, they indicate that the migrant sample includes a greater percentage. Compared with the 16 per cent of women in the sample who were divorced or separated, 7.2 per cent of all adult women in San Juan were so reported in 1940; in Ponce the figure is 2.8 per cent, and in Mayaguez 2.7 per cent.[8]

5

The migrant is likely to have had more formal schooling than the islander. The members of our sample have completed an average (median) of 6.5 years in school. The men have had a little more schooling than the women—median for men is 6.9 years, for women, 6.2 years.

TABLE II-6. PROPORTION IN EACH AGE GROUP WHO ARE ILLITERATE, NEW YORK MIGRANTS COMPARED WITH SAN JUAN AND INSULAR POPULATION

Age	New York migrants	San Juan[a]	Puerto Rico[a]
20–44 years[b]	3%	13%	28%
45 years and older	25%	36%	65%
All age groups	8%	17%	32%

[a] Source: U. S. Census, 1940. Puerto Rico, *Population*, Bulletin 2, p. 22.

[b] The migrants include those 18 and 19 years of age, which biases the results slightly downward.

Unfortunately, exact figures on the educational level of the islanders are not available for comparison, but there are strong indications that it is lower than for migrants. For instance, in our sample only 8 per cent were illiterate contrasted with 17 per cent in San Juan and 32 per cent on the whole island in 1940.

It is the older people who are less able to read and write. One fourth of the New York migrants 45 years old or older were illiterate, but figures for San Juan show illiteracy in over one third (36 per cent) of this group. Among the New York migrants

under 45 years of age, illiteracy is negligible—3 per cent; among
San Juan islanders of the same age group, 13 per cent were
illiterate in 1940.

The Puerto Rican migrants, although more educated than the
island population, are less educated than the general New York
population. Compared with the 8 per cent in our sample who
were illiterate, about 4.5 per cent of New York's population is
reported to be illiterate. Compared with six out of ten New
Yorkers who have had no more than eighth grade schooling, there
are almost eight out of ten migrants.[9]

The educational levels of men and women are equal, with
one notable exception: four per cent of the men but 11 per cent
of the women have had *no* formal schooling and, fully 90 per
cent of the illiterate group are women.

TABLE II-7. EDUCATIONAL LEVEL OF PUERTO RICAN MIGRANTS
IN NEW YORK CITY'S TWO CORE SETTLEMENTS BY AGE

	Age			
Education	*18–29*	*30–39*	*40–49*	*50 and over*
None	1%	3%	10%	32%
1–5 years grade school	18	35	40	43
6–8 years grade school	38	36	32	19
High school	40	25	17	4
College	3	1	1	2
TOTAL (100%)	(328)	(357)	(253)	(175)

White migrants have had more formal education than
the colored. This is true both for men and women, but the dis-
crepancy is more marked among women with one exception:
the same proportions of white and colored women never went
to school, but among the men relatively more of the colored than
the white have had no formal schooling.[10]

Educational attainments are closely associated with age: 19
per cent of those under 30, but 75 per cent of those 50 years of
age and over, have not gone beyond the fifth grade in school.

There is little educational difference between the recent and the early migrants to the city. More important than time of arrival are the demographic factors of sex, age, and race. The colored migrants of both sexes have had less education than the whites; in each race, women have had less schooling than men; the older migrants of both sexes and races are less educated than the younger ones.

TABLE II-8. MEDIAN YEARS OF SCHOOLING OF PUERTO RICAN MIGRANTS, BY SEX, AGE, AND RACE

	Men			Women		
Age	White	Colored	All men	White	Colored	All women
Under 35	7.6	7.1	7.4	7.3	5.5	7.2
35 or older	6.7	5.8	6.5	6.9	5.1	5.3
All age groups	7.1	6.3	6.9	6.5	4.4	6.2

In all groups, with the exception of the older white migrants among whom the women have had just as much or more education than the men, the men, the younger or the white migrants, will be better educated. However, among the men, age is more crucial to having a higher education than race; while among the women, race is more important than age.

6

Now a certain pattern of migration begins to emerge. The migration stream of Spanish Harlem and Morrisania includes a disproportionate share of women, particularly of divorced women and of Negroes and intermediates. The migrants seem to have had more formal schooling than the general island population. These selective patterns are closely related to the predominantly urban origin of the migrants in our sample. Generally, their urban residence on Puerto Rico was not a step in a journey from country to city to overseas voyage. In the main, they always lived in cities; only about one out of five can be considered rural in origin. The rest have merely changed the size and complexity of the city in which they live.

Ninety-one per cent of all persons in the sample had lived in the island's urban centers before coming to New York, compared with the 28 per cent of the total island population classified as urban in the 1940 census. Among the intermediate and Negro migrants there is the same high proportion of urban dwellers. About 92 per cent of the colored Puerto Rican migrants came from the cities, compared with 26.5 per cent of the general colored population who were city dwellers in 1940.[11]

The later migrants, particularly colored men and white women, tend to have been recruited more heavily from the island's rural areas. Five per cent of the men and 7 per cent of the women who came before 1942 were from rural areas in Puerto Rico, compared with 10 per cent of the more recently arrived men and 13 per cent of the recent women.[12]

But the island's two largest cities—San Juan and Ponce—supply the mainland with the majority of its migrants. Half of those who made the trip to New York came from the San Juan district, and twenty per cent of the migrants came from Ponce, Puerto Rico's second largest city.[13]

Whatever the period in which they made the journey, more of the Negro migrants than the white have tended to be recruited from the San Juan area. In both color groups, the more recent migrants are more apt to have come from San Juan than from Ponce.[14]

Considering the present high rate of internal migration in Puerto Rico, it might be supposed that the New York migrant lived in the island's metropolitan centers only for a short while. But this does not seem to be the case. For the most part, all groups of migrants come from a fairly stable population. About 80 per cent of the sample lived in one place during their last ten years on the island; only 2 per cent had moved during the year previous to their coming.

There is a further indication that the New York migrants were not a highly mobile group on the island: over half of the people interviewed had previously never moved at all and less than one third moved once. Only those 12 per cent who moved from their place of birth two or more times can in any sense be considered mobile.

7

The migrants' urban background is reflected again in their industrial history. The island's labor force is principally engaged in agricultural work; manufacturing and service industries are a relatively minor source of employment. But among the migrants, this is reversed. A very small proportion (5 per cent) had held agricultural jobs before coming to New York, although in 1947, 39 per cent of all insular jobs were in agriculture. Twice as many workers in manufacturing and processing are in the migrant group as in the whole working population of the island as of 1947.[15]

TABLE II-9. INDUSTRIAL SOURCE OF EMPLOYMENT IN PUERTO RICO OF MIGRANTS TO SPANISH HARLEM AND MORRISANIA, COMPARED WITH URBAN ISLAND POPULATION BY SEX

Last industry in Puerto Rico	Migrants		Urban workers in island labor force, 1940[a]	
	Men	Women	Men	Women
Agriculture	9%	1%	9%	1%
Manufacturing and processing[b]	29	68	28	38
Trade and transportation	23	4	39	8
Services[c]	39	27	24	53
TOTAL (100%)	(310)	(298)	(131,907)	(68,116)

[a] Source: U.S. Census, 1940, Puerto Rico, *Population*, Bulletin 2, p. 27.
[b] Includes 1 per cent employed in home industry.
[c] Includes government service.

Even compared with the island's urban labor force, the migrants are a selected group. The men in Spanish Harlem and Morrisania are almost twice as likely as the average male city

dweller in Puerto Rico to have worked in service industries and
less likely to have been in trade or transportation. The women,
on the other hand, and unlike urban women on the island, are
more likely to have worked in manufacturing and processing,
and less in the service industries.

Fifty-four per cent of the migrants (69 per cent of the men
and 37 per cent of the women) were in the labor force at the
time they left Puerto Rico; while on the island, 52 per cent of
the urban adult population in 1940 were working (75 per cent
of the men and 32 per cent of the women).[16] Thus, the women
migrants were slightly more apt to have worked than the average
urban islander; while the men were less likely to have been
working—probably due to the fact that many male migrants
came to New York just as they reached working age.

The migrant stream carries proportionately fewer unemployed
persons than in the island population: 4 per cent of the migrants
who were in the labor force in Puerto Rico reported that they
had been unemployed at the time they left the island, compared
with a range of from 11 to 20 per cent annual average in recent
years in Puerto Rico.[17] A relatively higher proportion of women
than men were unemployed when they left: 6 per cent of the
women as against 2 per cent of the men. Furthermore, of all those
who were employed on the island before they left, 71 per cent
had worked a full uninterrupted year in an economy marked by
sharp seasonal unemployment.

The island's skilled and semiskilled workers are being siphoned
off in greater numbers than their proportion in Puerto Rico's
labor force; less than half the island's "quota" of unskilled
migrants are coming to New York. On the island in 1940, 5 per
cent of the gainfully employed were classified as skilled workers;
in our sample 18 per cent had held skilled jobs. On the island,
20 per cent of the gainfully employed were classified as semiskilled workers in Puerto Rico's census; in our sample 41 per
cent had held semi-skilled jobs. Finally, half the island's labor
force were classified in 1940 as unskilled labor; among the

migrants, a little more than one fifth (21 per cent) had held
unskilled jobs.[18]

Although the variations between the races are slight, the
white men are the ones, on the island, who were more likely to
have done skilled or semiskilled work. White and Negro women,
if they held jobs at all, worked at nearly equivalent skill levels.

Yet, considering the predominantly urban origin of the
migrants, it is to be expected that more highly skilled workers
would leave the island. But only certain types of city dwellers
migrate from Puerto Rico. For example, white-collar workers,
particularly among the men, are represented in the migration to
a much lesser extent than they are in the island's urban labor
force.

TABLE II-10. OCCUPATIONAL CLASSIFICATION OF MIGRANTS TO SPANISH
HARLEM AND MORRISANIA WHO WERE GAINFULLY EMPLOYED IN
PUERTO RICO, COMPARED WITH THE URBAN LABOR FORCE BY SEX

Skill level of last job held in Puerto Rico	Migrants		Puerto Rican urban labor force[b]	
	Men	Women	Men	Women
White collar[a]	24%	17%	40%	23%
Skilled	19	16	16	*
Semiskilled	28	54	24	42
Unskilled	29	13	20	35
TOTAL (100%)	(308)	(313)	(131,907)	(68,116)

* Less than 1 per cent.
ᵃ "White collar" in this table, as in the other tables in this study, includes professional, semiprofessional, technical, small business or farm owners, and clerical
workers.
ᵇ Source: U. S. Census, 1940. Puerto Rico, *Population*, Bulletin 2, pp. 27 – 28.

Among the migrant men, the smaller proportion of white-
collar workers is accompanied by higher proportions of migrants
on every skill level of wage work. Compared with the urban labor
force, however, the women come in larger proportions from the
skilled and semiskilled levels.

Although the older male settlers were more likely than the

newer migrants to have been recruited from white-collar
occupations, the proportion who left such jobs on the island
even before 1942 does not approach the white-collar quota in
the island's urban labor force (28 per cent compared with 40
per cent). Probably as a result of wartime recruitment of labor,
the recently arrived men are more likely than those who came
before to have been skilled or semiskilled workers on the island.
Among these newcomers, the proportion who left skilled jobs in
Puerto Rico even exceeds the share of skilled workers in the
island's urban labor force (21 per cent of the newly arrived men
compared with 16 per cent of the men in the island's urban
labor force).

TABLE II-11. OCCUPATIONAL CLASSIFICATION OF MIGRANTS WHO WERE
GAINFULLY EMPLOYED IN PUERTO RICO, BY TIME OF ARRIVAL AND SEX

Skill level of last job held in Puerto Rico	Men		Women	
	Recent	Early	Recent	Early
White collar	19%	28%	20%	15%
Skilled	21	18	11	20
Semiskilled	33	22	57	51
Unskilled	27	32	12	14
TOTAL (100%)	(165)	(143)	(142)	(171)

Among the women, the older migrants were more likely to
have been skilled workers in Puerto Rico, while the newcomers
among the women are slightly more apt to have been white-
collar or semiskilled workers.

The migrants differ in still another way from the islanders in
the relatively better economic position they had in Puerto Rico.
Since they had held more highly skilled jobs than the average
islander their earnings in Puerto Rico were correspondingly
higher. Up to the beginning of the war, the migrants who were
then still working in Puerto Rico averaged about one fourth
more take-home pay than the island level. For their last job in
Puerto Rico, they report a median wage of $11.00 weekly, com-

pared with Puerto's median industrial wage during the prewar period of $9.00. During the war years, this margin narrowed considerably. Migrants who were still working in Puerto Rico in 1945 were earning no more than the average islander who worked in manufacturing or processing. The migrants averaged about $12.50 weekly, the Puerto Rican industrial worker about $12.00.[19]

This narrowing of the margin between the migrants' average wage and that of the total population was probably due to the impact of the war on the island's economy. Although war work led to full employment on the mainland, on the island it caused an increase in unemployment, and the rise in wages was less.[20]

8

The typical Puerto Rican migrant, living in New York City's Spanish Harlem or the lower Bronx, is 24 years of age, has completed about six years of schooling, comes from an urban area on the island and had always lived in such an area. The chances are six to four that the migrant is white, seven to three that she is married; we say "she" because it is six to four that the migrant is female. In the wage worker stratum, it is about even odds that the typical migrant worked as a semiskilled laborer in manufacturing or processing industries before making the journey. As a group, the migrants, in certain socially acquired characteristics, can be considered better fitted than stationary islanders for struggle on the continent. They are better educated; the women are more likely to be in the labor force. They are a source of labor supply for manufacturing and processing industries which require semiskilled and skilled workers. They reflect their predominantly urban, particularly San Juan, background, where most facilities for education, job experience, and training exist.

In many respects, compared with the islanders the migrants are more privileged than average. Yet—and this is of enormous importance to the fate of the Puerto Ricans in New York—many of the migrants are women, in a society where women's economic lot is still often difficult; many are Negroes, in a society in which color counts heavily against them; and most of the migrants—both Negro and white, both women and men—are without much skill, in a society where skill is increasingly important to adequate livelihood; and all enter a society where the opportunities for advancement seem increasingly to narrow for the poor, the uneducated, and the "foreign."

TWO:

THE JOURNEY

3. *Motivations*

THREE sets of factors play into the reasons for the Puerto Rican migration to New York City: the push from the homeland, the pull of the new country, and the sources of information about the new. In this migration, the crucial motivating force is the economic pull of the city; the island sources of information about the city are many and, in general, favorable—in fact, New York seems to have a monopoly on the vision of the place to go from Puerto Rico. Already inclined to leave because of the population pressure, manifested to the Puerto Rican by low living standards and lack of jobs, he is beckoned by the city's reputation for economic opportunity. It is this pull of New York rather than the squeeze on the island that manifestly figures most prominently in the mind of the migrant.

I

When the United States economy is working well, it acts as a magnet, drawing migrants from Puerto Rico; when the economy slumps, it loses its pulling power, and the Puerto Rican migration ebbs or even flows back to the island. From 1908 (the earliest date of accurate figures) to 1948, the correlation between the ups and downs of the physical volume of business activity on the continent and the waves and troughs of migration from Puerto Rico has the high coefficient of .73.[1]

In the early period of the depression of 1907, at least 8000 more persons returned to the island than came from it. During the recession of 1921–22 there was again a small reverse flow; and the depression of the early 1930's resulted in a net migration back to the island of 8694 in four years. During the recession of 1938 there was a substantial drop in the number of migrants coming to New York, but not a net return.[2]

The only important exception to the generally close relationship between the continental economy and the flow of migration occurred during World War II. Transportation was not then

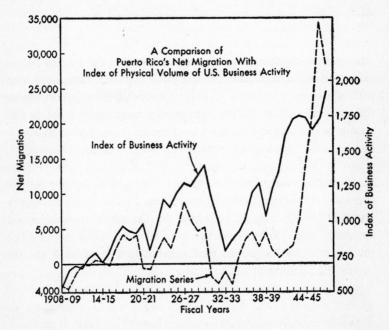

A Comparison of
Puerto Rico's Net Migration With
Index of Physical Volume of U.S. Business Activity

available, making it difficult for the islander to move. Toward the end of the war, however, the wave to New York started again when the War Manpower Commission recruited workers in Puerto Rico and sent them to the continent in army transports.

By the end of the war business began to boom in New York. Intense competition sprang up between passenger air lines anxious to service the island. Two companies maintained regular schedules and a score of nonschedule charter companies mushroomed almost overnight. Plane fare to New York, which had been $180, dropped to $75 on regular lines and as low as $35 on irregular.[3]

Under these conditions, the number of migrants reaching the continent shot up from 14,794 in 1944–45 to 34,405 in 1946–47, the peak postwar year, then dropped 19 per cent in 1947–48, with a total of 28,031 migrants.[4]

The correlation of migration and business cycles has generally held true of all migrations into the United States. Historically, immigration has played no specific part in intensifying United States unemployment, but rather has, as it were, been self-regulating. During times of American depression, immigration has slowed, halted, or even reversed itself. Just as the pull of United States conditions rather than the push of European conditions seems to have regulated the ebb and flow of European migrations,[5] so the Puerto Rican migration to New York City has regulated itself.*

2

In order to translate the objective facts of migration and the business cycle into psychological terms, it is necessary first to classify the migrants according to the role that the journey played in their lives. The person who independently made his decision to migrate and who also planned to stay in New York was making a different type of change in his life from a person who came because someone else did or one who initially planned only to visit the city. From such classifications, small children, brought by their families, are obviously excluded.**

"Did you or someone else decide to come to New York?" we asked the migrants. Some 54 per cent responded that they were the decision-makers; 46 per cent followed the decisions of others, the others being primarily family members already in New York.

More men than women are apt to make the decision to come to New York themselves; but among women, the older are more likely to have been deciders than followers. Here are the proportions of deciders according to age and sex:

* Cf. Chapter 2, section 1. Our sample tabulated by time of arrival follows the same pattern as the figures presented here.
** There were 105 cases in the sample who were too young at the time they left the island to participate in the decision. They are excluded from all the discussions in this chapter.

TABLE III-1. PROPORTION OF MIGRANTS IN EACH AGE AND
SEX GROUP WHO INDEPENDENTLY MADE THE DECISION
TO COME TO NEW YORK CITY[a]

Age	Men	Women	Total
35 and over	70%	45%	55%
18 to 35	74%	38%	52%
TOTAL	72%	42%	54%

[a] The figures in the table show only those proportions who made the decision to come. The difference between these figures and 100% gives the proportion who followed someone else's decision.

Whether the migrant made the journey alone or not, indicates in another way those who made the decision to migrate. Fifty-four per cent of the migrants made the trip to New York *alone*; 46 per cent came with others. Men were more apt to come alone than women, but among both men and women, the decision-makers were more likely to come alone than the followers. Here are the proportions who came to New York alone, according to their sex and whether or not they made the decision themselves.

TABLE III-2. PROPORTION WHO CAME TO NEW YORK ALONE,
ACCORDING TO WHETHER THEY WERE DECIDERS
OR FOLLOWERS AND SEX

	Deciders	Followers	Total
Men	80%	68%	76%
Women	54%	39%	45%
TOTAL	67%	44%	54%

Thus, 80 per cent of the men "deciders" but only 39 per cent of the women "followers" came to New York alone. In all, a decider is most likely to be a man who was in the labor force in Puerto Rico and came to New York by himself; the typical follower is a young woman who had no job in Puerto Rico and came to New York in the company of others.

When they left the island, most of the migrants planned to stay in New York permanently. About 78 per cent said they had come intending to stay in the city; 10 per cent had certain reservations about it; 11 per cent had come only for a visit; and only one per cent were undecided.

Once here, however, regardless of their original intentions, more Puerto Ricans intend to stay: now 82 per cent intend to remain in the city, 4 per cent express reservations, 6 per cent plan only to visit, and 8 per cent are undecided. These figures reveal certain changes of intention after the migrants had been in New York a while. Here are their present intentions compared with their intentions before coming to New York.

TABLE III-3. PRESENT AND ORIGINAL INTENTIONS OF MIGRANTS TO REMAIN IN NEW YORK

	Original Intention			
Present intention	Stay	Stay with reservations	Undecided	Visit
Stay	89%	63%	67%	57%
Stay with reservations	4	9	—	5
Undecided	5	19	11	15
Visit	2	9	22	23
TOTAL (100%)	(786)	(101)	(10)	(111)

Only 11 per cent of those who had planned to stay have changed their minds but 63 per cent of those who once had reservations about staying in New York, 67 per cent of those who were undecided, and 57 per cent of those who thought they would only visit, now definitely plan to stay.

Among the followers, planning to stay is in effect merely the carrying out of a previously established decision to stay; hence they are more likely to have come with the original intention of staying and less apt to change their minds from "stay" to "go." Ninety-two per cent of the followers, but 86 per cent of the leaders, came with the original intention of staying, and 90 per cent of the followers, but only 81 per cent of the deciders have always intended to remain in New York.

Among the men, 87 per cent of the deciders, and 86 per cent of the followers, have always intended to stay. For the men, followers and deciders, migration is more apt to be a decisive step in their life pattern than for the women. Generally, they think about it more, and in thinking it over, change their minds more.

TABLE III-4. PRESENT AND ORIGINAL INTENTION OF MIGRANTS TO REMAIN IN NEW YORK, BY LEADERSHIP AND SEX

Original and present intention[a]	Men		Women	
	Deciders	Followers	Deciders	Followers
Originally planned to stay and still plan to stay	87%	86%	82%	90%
Originally planned to visit; now plan to stay	6	4	11	6
Originally planned to visit and still do so	3	3	4	3
Originally planned to stay; now plan to visit	4	7	3	1
TOTAL (100%)	(277)	(111)	(261)	(356)

[a] Those who had reservations about staying are classified with those who plan to stay; those who were undecided, with those who plan to visit.

The women follow the same general pattern as the men as long as they participate in the decision to migrate. But the women followers are even less likely to change their minds: 82 per cent of the women who were deciders, but 90 per cent of those who were followers, stick to their original intention to stay. The followers are women who are completing the migration of a family.

So few people have changed their minds from staying to

leaving that it is impossible to arrive at reliable figures but there is some tendency for the colored migrants to be more prone to change their original intention from "stay" to "go." The intermediate and Negro migrants are also slightly more cautious than the whites about planning unreservedly to remain in New York.

Among both men and women, deciders and followers, the white migrants are more apt than the colored groups to have always planned to remain in New York. In spite of these differences, however, the dominant pattern is for the majority of all types of migrants to see their migration from the beginning as a permanent change. They make the journey from island to city with every intention of remaining here for the rest of their lives.

3

To determine the Puerto Ricans' motives for migrating, we asked them: "Can you tell me, in your own words, why you left Puerto Rico and came to New York?"[6] The answers to this question were analyzed in two ways: for the general content of the reasons expressed, and for reference to conditions in Puerto Rico (push) or in New York (pull).*

Two thirds of the group who had planned before migrating to remain permanently in New York told our interviewers that they had looked forward to bettering their economic position. They expected, they said, that the city would offer them or their families a job, or a better job; that here they would be able to make money, to raise their level of living. Almost half explained that their reasons for making the journey had to do with their family situation. Most of those in this category were responding to the pull of relatives already settled here but some wanted to escape or avoid difficult family situations on the island. Some migrants cited both economic and family reasons,

* The analysis of motivations for migrating which appears on the following pages deals only with those respondents who, at the time they left the island, were old enough to participate in the decision to leave, and who, at that time, viewed the step as a permanent migration rather than as a visit. Thus, the base of the total sample in sections 3 and 4 becomes 902 cases, 532 deciders and 370 followers.

others cited both or either in combination with further motivations, but these two—economic quest and family—stood out in the motivation pattern.

Other reasons mentioned by the migrants included their desire for special facilities which New York offers—schools, hospitals, medical care—or for certain cultural advantages of living in New York, and a few migrants said they were looking for adventure.

The type of reason for migrating varies most according to whether or not the migrant was a decider. The deciders tend to migrate for economic reasons, whereas the followers usually come to New York to join their families. Within each group, however, men tend to migrate for economic reasons, the women for family reasons.

TABLE III-5. REASONS FOR MIGRATING TO NEW YORK, BY SEX AND LEADERSHIP

Reasons for Migrating[a]	Deciders		Followers	
	Men	Women	Men	Women
Economic	89%	69%	62%	44%
Family	16	36	53	83
Special facilities	13	10	15	10
Cultural milieu	12	10	15	7
Hope of adventure	10	10	4	3
Other	2	2	1	1
TOTAL[b]	(277)	(240)	(69)	(291)

[a] The percentages add to more than 100 since some respondents gave more than one reason for migrating.
[b] Excludes 25 respondents for whom the reason of migration is not known.

Eighty-nine per cent of the men deciders, but only 44 per cent of the women followers migrated for economic reasons; whereas 83 per cent of the women followers, but only 16 per cent of the men deciders came for family reasons. This pattern of economic and family reasons holds for early as well as recent, colored as well as white, migrants.

But does a Puerto Rican decide to leave the island because he was pushed off, so to speak, by the pressures to which he was subject on the island, or, on the other hand, was he "pulled off" by hopes of special advantages in New York?

While it is true that the Puerto Rican would not be susceptible to the pull of New York unless there was some push in the migrant's subjective experience, the pull tends to be emphasized, the push minimized. As he sees it, it is this pull which affects his decision to leave the island. Of all the respondents who intended to stay in New York, about three quarters expressed their motivations in terms of the pull of New York, as against about one quarter who mentioned pressures on the island. The deciders are more likely, irrespective of sex, to have been pushed from the island.

TABLE III-6. PUSH-PULL MOTIVATION BY LEADERSHIP

Motivation[a]	Deciders	Followers	Total
Pull	67%	86%	75%
Push	27	20	24
Both	14	8	13
Neither	3	1	2
TOTAL[b]	(517)	(360)	(877)

[a] The percentages add to more than 100 since some respondents mentioned more than one reason for migrating and they may have been either pushed or pulled by either reason.

[b] Excludes 25 respondents whose motivation pattern is not known.

One major cause of these differences becomes clear when we cross-classify types of reason by push-pull factors.

Family reasons and the special facilities which New York offers (classed as "other") pull the migrant toward New York. Of those who give only family reasons, 90 per cent of the followers and 73 per cent of the deciders were pulled to New York to join their families, 23 per cent of the deciders were pushed off the island by family pressures, many of them being women who sought to escape family domination on the island.

Others who were pushed said that they were left alone either by the death of a spouse or some other kind of a family break-up, and that they looked upon the journey as an opportunity to escape the loneliness which in Puerto Rico they felt they would have to face.

TABLE III-7. PUSH-PULL BY REASONS FOR MIGRATION, AND LEADERSHIP

	Deciders				Followers			
Motivation[a]	Economic only	Economic and Family	Family only	Other	Economic only	Economic and Family	Family only	Other
Pushed	30%	31%	23%	4%	30%	41%	7%	—
Both pull and push	17	12	5	6	12	12	4	10
Pulled	60	89	73	80	62	97	90	92
Neither	13	—	—	10	1	1	1	—
TOTAL[b]	(338)	(65)	(64)	(50)	(80)	(90)	(166)	(24)

[a] Adds to more than 100% because some respondents mentioned more than one reason.
[b] Excludes 25 respondents whose motivation pattern is not known.

But no matter what the content of the reasons for migration, the great majority of the migrants felt that they were pulled to New York. Economic reasons, however, are more often experienced as a push from the island, while family reasons are associated with the experience of a pull to New York.

The migration of the Puerto Ricans to New York as a whole is to be seen, therefore, as an economic move, particularly among the deciders; their economic frustration on the island is less discernible, subjectively, to them than the rosy promise which they see in New York. New York beckons also to the followers; but they respond not so much to economic opportunity as to the pull exercised by their families already living here. Yet even their motivation has been indirectly economic. They are, after all, responding to the suggestion of some decider in the family, a decider who was most likely to have been economically motivated in making his original decision. Thus the followers are actually responding to *someone else's* economic motivation rather than their own.

When the deciders declare that they see their move to New York mainly as a response to the city's economic promise, they are, in effect, expressing their decision to search elsewhere for the better jobs, the opportunity, and the wages not accessible to them in Puerto Rico. When the followers explain their emotional and financial need to be with their families in New York, they too are expressing, though indirectly, their urge to find elsewhere the security which for them the island cannot provide. Yet, all these groups subjectively experience these impulses not as a deficiency of life on the island, but in terms of the advantages of the metropolis. There has been after all no drastic change in the life of the Puerto Rican, accustomed as he is to a chronically depressed economy. If anything, conditions there are continually improving. On the other hand, in the last twenty years the United States' economy has had periods of dazzling prosperity, and it is these dramatic peaks which beckon. They, rather than chronic deprivation on the island, monopolize the migrant's attention and seem to him to determine his course.

4

Economic pull could not operate unless there were sources of favorable information about New York City on the island. Puerto Rico is in fact permeated with influences of and, one might say, lures to the continental city. Almost all purchasable commodities are made in the United States; there is in San Juan "The New York Department Store"; the school texts printed in the United States tell the children about the mainland; a large proportion of families in Puerto Rico has relatives or friends in New York; and over all spheres of life on the island there looms an image of the city.

So pervasive is this New York atmosphere, especially in the Puerto Rican cities from which the migrants come, that it is not curious that those who finally did come spent little time pondering the decision: 37 per cent said they had thought out the idea of migrating in less than one month, another 38 per cent for more than a month but less than one year, only 25 per cent are aware that it took them one year or more to make up their minds to come.

More of the deciders, both men and women, ponder the idea longer than the followers; among the followers, women waited longer than men. This holds true of all color groups. Those who come for economic reasons took longer to decide than those who migrated for family reasons.

Since the social atmosphere of Puerto Rico is so pervaded by lures to New York, there is little dependence upon formal media (newspapers, magazines, radio, movies, travel posters, or recruiting bulletins) to inform the Puerto Ricans about it. Fully 81 per cent of the migrants referred to informal, face-to-face contact as their single most important source of information—conversations with, and letters from, friends or relatives who were living in or had visited the city. Formal media of information were mentioned by only 14 per cent, while 5 per cent had obtained their information by previous personal visits to New York. This holds true for both men and women, for both deciders and followers, and for all racial groups.

Not all migrants, however, depended upon the same type of informal media. Of all those whose single most important source of information is informal media (conversation and letters), here are the proportions who depended upon letters:

TABLE III-8. PROPORTION DEPENDING ON LETTERS OF THOSE WHOSE MOST IMPORTANT SOURCE OF INFORMATION WAS INFORMAL MEDIA, BY SEX AND LEADERSHIP

	Deciders	Followers	Total
Men	51%	68%	54%
Women	61%	89%	75%
TOTAL	56%	84%	67%

Regardless of sex, more followers than deciders depended upon letters; and, in both classes, more women than men. That more followers, and particularly more women, came to join families already in New York makes it clear that they would have to hear about New York through letters from their families already there.

It is of further interest to see to what extent these informal means are available to the migrants. In addition to asking for the single main source of their information, we asked the respondents whether they had received information about New York from letters, what people told them, or what they asked people about—and in each case whether the information was from family members or friends. About three quarters of the migrants received letters; about the same percentage were told about life in New York City by family members and friends who had been there, and about 40 per cent asked others about it.

More deciders than followers were exposed to information through what people told them or what they asked people; while more followers than deciders received information about New York from letters. Among the deciders more received information from letters from family members (52 per cent) than from what family members told them (25 per cent); the same general finding is true among the followers. Conversation about New York seems to have taken place among friends, while correspondence took place with relatives. This is especially true among the followers, as we have already seen: 75 per cent of them received letters from family members. As the deciders are people for whom the migration is usually a decisive economic step, they are less dependent for information from families—regardless of whether through correspondence or conversation.[7]

Women, regardless of whether they are followers or deciders, follow the general pattern of the followers in these respects; while the men, regardless of whether or not they made their own decision to migrate, follow the patterns outlined by the deciders.

These statements only illustrate the sources of information

open to the migrants. How decisive these influences of informal media were in actually drawing the migrant towards New York we cannot say, since we have no way to determine how much those Puerto Ricans who did *not* migrate were exposed to these same sources of information.

5

Under the conditions described above, it is almost inevitable that the atmosphere of the island is strongly oriented toward New York City. Although there do exist scattered settlements of Puerto Ricans in other sections of the country, the greatest concentration has always been in New York. In 1910 over half of all Puerto Ricans living in the States lived in New York, in 1920, 79 per cent, and in 1940, 95 per cent.[8]

Compared with New York, other scattered settlements of Puerto Ricans in the States have only very weak pulling power. In response to the question, "Back on the island, when you were thinking of leaving Puerto Rico, did you ever consider the idea of going to some other place except New York City?" 89 per cent of the migrants said they had never considered any other place; 11 per cent said they had considered the idea but had given it up. We then asked both groups, "If for some reason it had been impossible for you to come to New York City, what would you have done?" Some 83 per cent asserted that they would have stayed in Puerto Rico; more women than men said so, and, in each sex group, a few more followers than deciders. This substantiates the over-all finding that most of the people who consider leaving the island think specifically of coming to New York City and never seriously consider any other place.

6

When the Puerto Rican is ready to leave the island, he is psychologically prepared to move into one of the Puerto Rican colonies of New York City. Because many of his friends or relatives are already in the metropolis, it seems easy to make the hop from San Juan to LaGuardia Field. Once in the city, he usually settles down to stay.

The main pattern of the Puerto Rican migration to New York City consists simply of one direct trip. Two deviant patterns, both of small scale, nevertheless deserve brief examination: (A) One we call the New York trial migrant: this person moves to New York, gives up the idea of remaining, returns to Puerto Rico, but again comes to New York. (B) The other is also a trial migrant but his first migration is not to New York City; he left Puerto Rico to settle elsewhere; returned to the island; and later came to New York.

(A) Of all the migrants who were adults when they left Puerto Rico, only 101, or 10 per cent, had been to New York previous to their settlement here; of these, 23 migrants had previously come only to visit, leaving 78 people who had been New York trial migrants, 8 per cent.

(B) Migrants who had been elsewhere on previous trips, excluding a few Army personnel and visitors, number 72 cases. These are about evenly split between those who first went somewhere else in the United States and those who went to some place outside the United States.

Both these trial migrant types differ substantially from their countrymen who settle on their first trip to New York; and each differs from the other. The migrant who tried New York is a more independent agent; when he leaves, he does so for his own reasons. The migrant who tries elsewhere is less an independent agent and seems to be motivated mainly by objective economic circumstances. Practically all the New York trial migrants were deciders; 45 out of the 72 of the other trial migrants were.

The New York trial migrant is more likely to leave New York for family reasons and less likely to leave because his job is terminated or unsatisfactory, whereas trial migrants who did not try New York first were more apt to leave for economic reasons. The main reasons for trial migrations of both types were to fulfill job contracts or to seek work.

7

Of the relatively small number of Puerto Ricans (9–12 per cent) who say they are thinking about leaving New York, almost all think of returning to Puerto Rico, rather than moving else-where. Any movement is almost exclusively back and forth, and sex, race, or who made the decision do not affect it.

Those who plan or think about leaving New York are about evenly divided between those who feel pulled back to the island and those who are pushed from New York City. Those who feel pulled toward the island plan to return to Puerto Rico be-cause of a job there or a family expecting them.

TABLE III-9.   INTENTIONS OF MIGRANTS TO REMAIN IN OR LEAVE NEW YORK,
BY SEX AND LEADERSHIP

	Deciders		Followers	
	Men	Women	Men	Women
Will remain in New York	88%	91%	90%	89%
Never think of going elsewhere	71	76	71	78
Think of going back to Puerto Rico	10	8	10	8
Think of going elsewhere	7	7	9	3
Will not remain in New York	12%	9%	10%	11%
Elsewhere	1	2	1	1
Back to Puerto Rico	11	7	9	10
TOTAL[a] 100%	(267)	(240)	(68)	(291)

[a] Excludes 39 cases who did not answer either question, in addition to 103 cases who originally came only to visit.

The other half, those pushed from New York, have tried their luck here and found it wanting. For the most part, it is not an inability to get along economically in New York that makes them want to leave, but rather the general cultural milieu in the city that is unsatisfactory. Almost all who feel pushed from New York refer to the limitations on real aspirations here, the difficulties of bringing up children properly, and the impossibility of finding peace of mind in New York.

About three quarters of the migrants now plan to stay in New York *and* never think of going elsewhere.

As far as remaining in or leaving New York is concerned, there are few or no differences between deciders and followers, or between men and women. Once they are in the city, they are alike in their intention to stay.

The facts that economic pull to New York is the major motivating force of the migration and that, despite hardships in New York, which we shall consider later, the economic situation here does not prompt any return, point up the meaning of this migration in the experience of the people involved. That meaning lies in the occupational, income, and industrial spheres of their biographies; theirs is an economic transit.

4. *Economic Transit*

NEARLY three-fourths of the Puerto Rican migrants look forward to finding work upon their arrival in New York; about one fourth expect to go to school or to become housewives. Of course, more men than women expect to find work at the end of their journey: 83 per cent of the men, 63 per cent of the women.[1]

New York City attracts the Puerto Rican migrants by its promise of jobs; but to those who are already working on the island this pull is greater than to others. The typical migrant is not so much in search of a job as of a better job.

About 50 per cent of the migrants were in the labor force when they left Puerto Rico and expected to work when they arrived in New York City. Another 22 per cent were not working in Puerto Rico but expected to go to work upon their arrival in New York. Only 6 per cent were working in Puerto Rico but did not expect to work in New York; some 22 per cent were not working in Puerto Rico and did not come to New York with the expectation of working.

A small proportion of the men (3 per cent) were in the labor force in Puerto Rico but did not intend to work in New York. These were most frequently men who left jobs in Puerto Rico to come to New York to study; others worked in Puerto Rico but expected to enter the Army upon coming to New York. A small proportion of the men were too young to work in Puerto Rico and expected to continue in school upon arriving in New York; while others had just reached working age and left the island for jobs in New York.

Thirty-eight per cent of the women worked in Puerto Rico

and expected to work in New York. Six per cent were working on the island but expected to become housewives in New York; but 27 per cent were not working on the island but expected to work in New York.

TABLE IV-1. EMPLOYMENT STATUS IN PUERTO RICO AND EXPECTED EMPLOYMENT STATUS IN NEW YORK, BY SEX

Status in Puerto Rico	Expected Status in New York	Men	Women	Total
In labor force	Work	74%	38%	50%
In labor force	Not work	3	6	6
Not in labor force	Work	14	27	22
Not in labor force	Not work	9	29	22
TOTAL (100%)[a]		(408)	(667)	(1075)

[a] Excludes 9 men and 29 women who did not answer both questions.

That an unknown proportion of working-age Puerto Ricans on the island leave for jobs in New York is indicated by the fact that fewer migrants were in the labor force when they left Puerto Rico than the number who leave expecting to work in New York. Women particularly seem to prefer working in New York rather than in Puerto Rico. Only a little more than four out of ten of the women migrants were working or seeking work when they left the island but better than six out of ten came to New York with the idea of finding jobs. Thus, among the women there were some 21 per cent who were reluctant to work on the island but who were willing to work in New York. These were mostly housewives but a few were school girls who, when they were ready to enter the labor market, felt that New York provided a better opportunity for them. The willingness of these housewives to work in New York but not in Puerto Rico is partly due to a status difference between the island and mainland; as one woman migrant told us: "You know how it is on the island. If you work you can hold only a certain kind of job or people look down on you." In New York they find a difference: "Here it is no disgrace for a woman to work at any kind of job, even if it is in a factory. Everyone does it."

I

The migrants generally come to New York expecting to work, yet few of them have specific expectations about the kind of work they will do. Of those expecting to find work in the city, only 20 per cent have any special type of work in mind; a few, 2 per cent, have jobs lined up before they leave Puerto Rico; 2 per cent are planning to carry on their own business, 8 per cent to work and study; while 68 per cent come to New York looking for any kind of work they can get.

The women who planned to seek work in New York are less likely than the men to have planned on a special type of work. Seventy-one per cent of the women who expected to work, as against 65 per cent of the men, would take any job. Nearly one fourth of the men, but 17 per cent of the women, were seeking some special kind of work.[2]

Clearly, looking for a job is one of the first steps the new migrant takes. Adding to the usual difficulties in finding work in a strange city, these people frequently do not know the language, or, if they do know it, are afraid or embarrassed to use it. The migrants are reluctant to use job-getting agencies. Only about 4 per cent secured their first jobs in New York this way. Few of them know about the state employment services, and they are highly suspicious of the private agencies they do know about. Most Puerto Ricans would agree with one man who said: "Those agencies are rackets. They get you a job for a week and you pay them, then you get fired and they get someone else the same job and they get paid again." Nor do they simply accept the difficulties: "There should be an office in New York to help Puerto Ricans get jobs. Our people come here and everyone takes advantage of them. There should be a government office to help them find work."

It is to friends and relatives already at work that the migrants turn: 76 per cent got their first job in the city in this way, 14 per cent relied on their own efforts, and 10 per cent turned to agencies or newspaper ads. But after they have been here a while, they rely less upon friends and relatives and more upon their "own efforts"; only 58 per cent got their present jobs through friends and relatives, while 26 per cent got them on their own and 16 per cent through formal agencies or formal media.

2

Most of the migrants who were in the labor force in Puerto Rico before they came to New York have at one time or another entered the New York labor force: 95 per cent of the men and 82 per cent of the women.[3]

TABLE IV-2. LABOR FORCE STATUS[4] BETWEEN LAST
JOB IN PUERTO RICO AND FIRST JOB IN NEW YORK,
BY SEX

	Men	Women
Entered labor force	15%	36%
Always in	79	41
Left labor force	4	9
Never in	2	14
TOTAL[a] (100%)	(362)	(640)

[a] For this table, and those following in this chapter, the total cases represent only those workers for whom we had information on both questions involved; the total cases, therefore, vary slightly from table to table.

As a great majority of the men were working when they left Puerto Rico, for them the migration meant a transfer from one job to another: 79 per cent of all men did this. Fifteen per cent of the men were too young to work in Puerto Rico but entered the labor force in New York City. Only six per cent were not in the labor force in either place, or left the labor force upon arriving in New York.

For many women, however, the migration to New York has meant an initial entry into the labor force.

Some 36 per cent of the women migrants had never worked in Puerto Rico but took a job or started to look for one when they came to New York. For the most part, these were house-wives on the island who left Puerto Rico in order to gain the economic and social freedom which they felt New York offered them; many are divorcées and widows who came without their families, expecting to support themselves; a few were young girls who had just reached working age at the time of their migration.

Once in New York, the men continue working and thus stay in the labor force, but quite a few women stop working and revert to housewife status.

TABLE IV-3. LABOR FORCE STATUS BETWEEN FIRST
AND PRESENT JOBS IN NEW YORK, BY SEX

	Men	Women
Always in	84%	41%
Left labor force	11	36
Never in	5	23
TOTAL (100%)	(382)	(657)

Eighty-four per cent of the men, but only 41 per cent of the women, have remained in the New York labor force—36 per cent of the women, but only 11 per cent of the men, had at one time worked in New York but are no longer in the labor force.

Thus, from the time they left Puerto Rico until now, most men have been continually in the labor force. Many women, however, enter the labor force for the first time when they reach New York, and then leave it after being here for a while. From the time they left Puerto Rico until the present, the economic movement of the migrants, in and out of the labor force, may be summed up as in table IV-4.

Except for young men who reach the working age upon their arrival in New York, the men remain continually in the labor force. The women form no such pattern: those who worked in Puerto Rico are now just as apt to be in the labor force as out of it—23 per cent remained in, and 26 per cent were in when they left Puerto Rico but are no longer. Similarly, those who did not work in Puerto Rico are almost as likely to work here as not.

TABLE IV-4. LABOR FORCE STATUS BETWEEN LAST JOB IN PUERTO RICO AND PRESENT JOB IN NEW YORK

	Men	Women
Entered labor force	16%	20%
Always in	69	23
Left labor force	11	26
Never in labor force	4	31
TOTAL	(395)	(674)

Such patterns do not hold true for all color groups. Among both men and women the colored migrants, especially the Negroes, are more apt than the whites to have always been in the labor force.

TABLE IV-5. LABOR FORCE STATUS FROM LEAVING PUERTO RICO TO PRESENT, BY SEX AND RACE

	Men			Women		
	White	Int.	Negro	White	Int.	Negro
Entered labor force	19%	8%	9%	22%	17%	17%
Always in	68	71	78	20	24	31
Left labor force	10	17	10	25	30	25
Never in	3	4	3	33	29	27
TOTAL (100%)	(280)	(54)	(59)	(404)	(114)	(156)

Only 8 or 9 per cent of the colored men were too young to work or were students in Puerto Rico but worked for the first time when they came to New York, in contrast to 19 per cent of the white men. Among women, the proportions who entered the labor force in New York are roughly similar for all racial groups, but there are more students and fewer housewives who enter the labor force in New York among the whites. Furthermore, white women, more than colored, remain housewives, not working in Puerto Rico or in New York.

3

Most Puerto Rican migrants are wage workers. If they worked before leaving the island, they held more or less skilled wageworker jobs. Some 20 per cent had been in the white-collar occupations: professional or semiprofessional, owners of small businesses or farms, or clerical workers. The remaining 80 per cent had held handwork jobs, ranging from spot welder to stevedore, busboy to flower-maker. Some 18 per cent were skilled, 41 per cent semiskilled, and 21 per cent unskilled.

When the migrants arrive in New York, they are even more concentrated in hand worker occupations: the first job of some 89 per cent is wagework; 18 per cent on the skilled level, 25 per cent semiskilled, and 46 per cent unskilled. Only 11 per cent enter white-collar jobs. A definite occupational downgrading seems to be involved in their first job in New York.

After they have been here a while, they do begin slowly to raise their occupational standing. This rise takes place more within the skill levels of the wageworker stratum than between this stratum and the white-collar world. Only 12 per cent of the migrants living in the core settlements, regardless of length of time in New York, now hold white-collar positions. Within the wageworker stratum, however, there are now about as many who are working on the skilled level as on the island—15 per cent— and there are many more on the semiskilled—53 per cent—and correspondingly, fewer on the unskilled—only 20 per cent.

The men are less occupationally concentrated than the women, both in Puerto Rico and in New York. Even though the male dispersion in occupation is not very wide, they have more opportunities for different kinds of work than do women. They are more likely to hold white-collar jobs or become small businessmen, both on the island and in New York: 24 per cent of the men, and 17 per cent of the women had such jobs in Puerto Rico. Once in New York, both men and women drop out of the white-collar world.

Although Puerto Rico is exporting a higher proportion of skilled and semiskilled workers to the mainland than the island proportion, the migrants are by no means comparable with the New York population in level of skill. Men in New York City's labor forces are split about 50-50 between white-collar and wageworker jobs; all but 15 per cent of the Puerto Rican men migrants work for wages. Even on the island, where more men held white-collar jobs, only 24 per cent did so.

TABLE IV-6. COMPARISON BETWEEN THE SKILL LEVEL OF ALL EMPLOYED PUERTO RICAN MIGRANTS IN NEW YORK CITY AND OF ALL EMPLOYED WORKERS IN NEW YORK CITY, BY SEX

	Men			Women		
	Migrant Labor Force			Migrant Labor Force		
Occupation	Last Job in P. R.	Present Job in N. Y.	N. Y. Labor Force[a]	Last Job in P. R.	Present Job in N. Y.	N. Y. Labor Force[a]
White collar	24%	15%	45%	17%	9%	56%
Wageworkers	76	85	55	83	91	44
Skilled	19	24	17	16	5	1
Semiskilled	28	36	15	54	73	21
Unskilled	29	25	23	13	13	22
TOTAL (100%)	(308)	(362)		(313)	(248)	

[a] The classfication of the New York City labor force by skill level is taken from C. Wright Mills, *The New Middle Class* (Oxford University Press, to be published, 1951).

The same contrast, as seen among the men, exists between the skill level of the New York women at work and that of the migrant working women. A little less than half of all women working in New York City are classified in wagework, but all except 9 per cent of the Puerto Rican women migrants now work in such jobs. On the island, all but 17 per cent had held such wageworker jobs.

Puerto Rico's economy is pre-white collar, still in the peasant and artisan stage. Only in an advanced society do the tertiary occupations, the white-collar jobs, become widely available. The difference is that between a colonial society, with its white-collar stratum of petty officials, and a mature capitalist society, with its enlarged white-collar worlds.

4

Occupational concentration among the Puerto Ricans in the New York core settlements is paralleled by industrial concentration. Both on the island and in New York the migrants consistently cluster in the manufacturing and processing industries. Almost half of those who were working before they left Puerto Rico (47 per cent) held jobs in these industrial groups. At first, in New York, the proportion rises to 61 per cent of the gainfully employed, later declines slightly to 56 per cent.

The same parallel prevails for those employed in the service trades and in domestic service jobs. One fifth of the gainfully employed on the island (20 per cent) worked in these trades. When they arrive in New York, the proportion who secure such jobs rises to 30 per cent and remains stable.[5]

In large part responsible for the industrial concentration of New York Puerto Ricans is the fact that the migrants who worked in agriculture, government, or retail or wholesale trade on the island, in New York go into the manufacturing or service industries; whereas those migrants who worked in the manufacturing or service trades on the island have in New York remained in these industrial groups.

5

Puerto Rican newcomers can hardly be choosy about their first job in New York; they remain on or drop down to low-level jobs, and any later rise in job level is most likely to occur among those who were formerly in the lowest occupation. Whatever upward mobility has occurred in the job life of the Puerto Rican migrants is largely restricted to the climb from unskilled to semiskilled wagework. Many, but by no means all, of the migrants, at first unable to find equivalent jobs in New York, do eventually return to their island status.

Of those migrants who were at work in Puerto Rico and who entered the labor force in New York upon their arrival, nearly one half of them, 45 per cent of the men and 51 per cent of the women, took jobs in New York at the same level of skill at which they worked on the island. Most of these men were unskilled workers, while the women were more apt to be semiskilled.

TABLE IV-7. LAST OCCUPATION IN PUERTO RICO TO FIRST OCCUPATION IN NEW YORK, BY SEX[6]

Direction of mobility	Men	Women
Upward	13%	15%
Stable	45	51
Downward	42	34
TOTAL (100%)	(265)	(258)

Over one third of the migrants experience downward job mobility, taking jobs at lower skill levels than they held on the island. Among the men, most of the white-collar and skilled workers, and about half of the semiskilled, took lower level jobs in New York; among the women, most of the white-collar and skilled. Only 13 per cent of the men and 15 per cent of the women moved upward; and these few were mainly, among both men and women, unskilled workers in Puerto Rico finding semiskilled jobs in New York.

Once they are in New York very few migrants rise above the level of their first job here. Many migrants of course remain stable—higher proportions than on the jump from Puerto Rico to their first job in New York—but considerable proportions continue to experience downward job mobility.

TABLE IV-8. FIRST OCCUPATION IN NEW YORK TO
PRESENT OCCUPATION IN NEW YORK, BY SEX

Direction of mobility	Men	Women
Upward	29%	12%
Stable	50	74
Downward	21	14
TOTAL (100%)	(311)	(265)

After they have been here a while, the men begin to climb back, approximating their occupational levels on the island, the women remain at the semiskilled level; for any substantial rise between different jobs in New York is most likely to occur among the men. A few men on all levels of wagework in New York rise above their first job, but the largest share of the 29 per cent who rise is made up of migrants who were semiskilled workers on the island who took unskilled work in New York at first, and have since risen to semiskilled work. The women are much less apt to rise above the level of their first job here, the few who do rise, like the men, from unskilled to semiskilled, but the majority remaining stable. Among both men and women sizable proportions are now working at jobs below the level of skill of their first job in New York.

TABLE IV-9. FIRST OCCUPATION IN NEW YORK TO PRESENT OCCUPATION IN
NEW YORK, BY SEX AND TIME OF ARRIVAL

Direction of mobility	Men		Women	
	Early	Recent	Early	Recent
Upward	42%	15%	11%	12%
Stable	38	63	75	73
Downward	20	22	14	15
TOTAL (100%)	(144)	(167)	(122)	(143)

The longer the men are in New York, the more apt they are to move upward, but for the women length of residence in New York does not help them move upward in the world of jobs.

Forty-two per cent of the men who have been in New York for the longer periods of time, but only 15 per cent of the recent male arrivals, have moved upward while here; but time of arrival does not appreciably affect the proportions who move downward. Thus, the longer the male migrant is here, the more chance he has to rise; but the fact that some men rise after a period of time does not reduce the proportion who continue to move downward.

When the over-all situation is examined, from leaving Puerto Rico to present job in New York, it can be seen that the most important occupational shift has been a cumulative downward mobility. Forty per cent of both men and women are now working at jobs lower than those they held on the island before coming to New York.

TABLE IV-10. LAST OCCUPATION IN PUERTO RICO TO PRESENT OCCUPATION IN NEW YORK, BY SEX

Direction of mobility	Men	Women
Upward	21%	17%
Stable	39	43
Downward	40	40
TOTAL (100%)	(261)	(142)

An equivalent proportion of the migrants have succeeded in equalling the level of the job they had held in Puerto Rico, while only 21 per cent of the men, and 17 per cent of the women have experienced upward mobility.

In a limited sense, white men have a slight edge over Negroes. In their first jobs in New York, the white men's advantage tends to disappear, but after they have been here a while their chance for more skilled occupations may rise, while the Negroes are likely to remain in semiskilled jobs.

Comparing the present job in New York with the last job in Puerto Rico, the white men are more apt than the colored to experience upward mobility, but they are also more likely to experience downward mobility: in Puerto Rico the white men were in the more highly skilled jobs, which they were unable to equal in New York. The colored male migrants, both intermediate and Negro, have thus been relatively more stable, holding semiskilled and unskilled jobs both in Puerto Rico and in New York. Thus, although the white men have a better opportunity to move upward than the Negro, many (44 per cent) are still unable to equal the skill levels they left on the island.

TABLE IV-11. LAST OCCUPATION IN PUERTO RICO TO PRESENT OCCUPATION IN NEW YORK, BY SEX AND RACE

Direction of mobility	Men			Women		
	White	Int.	Negro	White	Int.	Negro
Upward	22%	16%	18%	16%	24%	14%
Stable	34	57	47	44	60	36
Downward	44	27	35	40	16	50
TOTAL (100%)	(178)	(37)	(45)	(73)	(25)	(44)

Among the women, the intermediates are more likely than either the Negroes or the Whites to stay at the same job level. This is probably due to the fact that they, more than any other group, enter New York as marginals; they, even more than the white and Negro women, stick to the same semiskilled jobs in New York as they held in Puerto Rico. From this position very little downward mobility is possible as long as they continue to work.

The downward occupational mobility which many migrants experience in the economic transit from island to continent is often not new in their lives. A considerable number had already been working at jobs below the level of their fathers' strata before they left Puerto Rico.

Thirty-four per cent of the men and 37 per cent of the women who reported on their father's occupation had already experienced a drop from the level of their father's job before coming to New York; more women than men had risen above the level of their father's job. In fact, the women are much more likely than the men to have moved, up or down, from the level of their father's job; many women were working at semiskilled jobs on the island, while their fathers, like the men migrants in our present sample, were more likely to have been either skilled or unskilled workers, rather than semiskilled.

TABLE IV-12. FATHER'S OCCUPATION TO MIGRANT'S LAST JOB IN PUERTO RICO, BY SEX OF MIGRANT[7]

Direction of mobility	Men	Women
Upward	32%	42%
Stable	34	21
Downward	34	37
TOTAL (100%)	(244)	(213)

In short, occupational mobility of the Puerto Ricans in New York is quite restricted: they are concentrated in lower skilled jobs, and their chances to rise above them seem rather slim. In the journey to New York, most of the migrants do not experience a rise in the level of their job, many in fact are now at lower levels than they held in Puerto Rico. For some, this downward mobility is a new experience, for others it is a continuation of a downward mobility already experienced on the island from the occupational position of their fathers. Still others, who have risen in jobs in coming to New York, have only regained the job status once held by their fathers.[8]

6

Although the jobs available to the Puerto Rican migrant are restricted mainly to semiskilled and unskilled jobs in the city's factories, hotels, restaurants, and other service trades, and although the chances of any occupational rise are slight, unquestionably the migrant is immediately able to better his income position. Average earnings in New York are considerably higher than those reported by the migrants who worked in Puerto Rico, and they have continued to increase as migrants gain job experience in New York and as they have benefited by the general wage rise on the continent.

The migrant's first job in New York doubles his former earnings. Not only does the average wage increase, but the income spread becomes wider. About three fourths of those employed in Puerto Rico earned under $20 weekly there; but for their first job in New York, only 34 per cent worked at that wage level. Forty per cent now earn $40.00 or more per week, compared to the 4 per cent earning that before coming to New York.[9] Although women consistently earn less money than men, they increase their earnings in New York at approximately the same rate. The present wage in New York (1948) is $42.70 for the men and $37.50 for the women.

TABLE IV-13. PRESENT MEDIAN WAGES[a] OF PUERTO RICAN MIGRANTS
by OCCUPATIONAL LEVEL, SEX AND RACE

Occupational Level	Men			Women		
	White	Colored	Total	White	Colored	Total
White collar	$57	$53	$55	$38	*	$42
Skilled	48	46	48	42	*	35
Semiskilled	48	40	45	35	35	35
Unskilled	36	37	37	33	26	29

[a] Median computed to nearest dollar.
* The cases are too few to allow reliable calculation of median wage.

Wage levels are related to occupational skills as well as to status position. The few Puerto Rican workers in the white-collar and the skilled occupations earn the highest wages; those in unskilled jobs, the lowest; those in semiskilled work are in between.

Even in the same occupation, Puerto Rican men earn consistently more than women, white more than colored. On every skill level, the differences in earnings between white and colored men are sharper than the differences between white and colored women.

As might be expected, the longer the migrant has been in New York, the more likely, on the average, he is to earn a higher income now. This correlation between income and length of residence holds true in general for all levels of skill.

TABLE IV-14. PRESENT MEDIAN WEEKLY WAGES OF
PUERTO RICAN MIGRANTS, BY SEX, RACE, AND
TIME OF ARRIVAL

Time of Arrival	Men		Women	
	White	Colored	White	Colored
Prewar II	$50	$50	$35	$32
World War II	45	43	35	31
Postwar II	43	31	26	32

In terms of income, as well as industry and occupation, the Puerto Ricans in New York are a rather homogeneous group. Between colored and white men there is little difference in earning capacity, except among the postwar arrivals where the white men have a slight advantage. The upward trend of earned income, associated with length of residence, holds true for every race and sex group except the colored women. Although recently arrived colored women are able to earn more money than recently arrived white women, the former are less able to improve their earning power.

It must be kept in mind, of course, that the migrants have increased their earnings during a period of economic inflation, when wages have risen, but the purchasing power of the dollar has been substantially lowered. Yet, regardless of when the migrant arrived, he has, on the average, very soon raised his earning power above island levels.

The average (median) weekly cash income of those migrants who came during the prosperity years prior to 1929 from the island's labor force, and who got jobs in New York was:

last job in Puerto Rico, $10.90

first job in New York, $20.70

Median earnings of those who came during the depression years of the 1930's were:

last job in Puerto Rico, $11.00

first job in New York, $21.90

Earnings for those who came during the war years were:

last job in Puerto Rico, $11.80

first job in New York, $31.24

The corresponding earnings for those who came during the postwar years were:

last job in Puerto Rico, $12.50

first job in New York, $32.20

Apparently this immediate and continual rise in money income serves to compensate the migrants for the downward job movement which they experience in New York. For they do not express any conscious dissatisfaction. As we shall see, when they are asked to express what job they would prefer to hold, over half of the migrants are unable to articulate even the wish for a different occupational status. This holds true for those who are already working, as well as for those who are not now in the labor force.

Within the New York job world, Puerto Rican mobility is limited. If it occurs at all, it is mainly a rise from unskilled to semiskilled jobs. The economic transit of the migrants means, on the whole, an increased money income that has to cover more cash expenditures, without appreciable occupational rise. But there are other worlds in the city into which the Puerto Ricans move and there are other meanings of their journey to the city of migrations.

THREE:

THE CITY

5.   *City of Migrations*

As ESTABLISHED by law, the Puerto Rican is an American, but the contrast between his rural island with its Spanish heritage and the American metropolis makes him, in psychological and cultural reality, a foreigner in the city. The country to which he comes is the classic country of immigrations; since 1820, it has been the destination of 61 per cent of all the immigrants in the world.[1] During the last century and a quarter, over 38 million immigrants have come to America, and in the entire country no place of reception has equaled New York City.[2]

New York is a city built by migrations. Time and again its streets and slums have been flooded by people from foreign lands. Even in 1940, over one quarter of New York's population was foreign-born,[3] and many more were the children of foreign-born parents. The lower east side is the world of the Russian and Polish Jew; east of 3rd Avenue, from Sutton Place uptown to Harlem, of the Italian; in Yorkville, of the German; and off the Bowery, on and around Mott Street, of the Chinese.

Each successive wave of migration has been met by various kinds of rhetoric. Newspapers and welfare workers, immigration authorities and politicians have vied with one another in casting aspersions upon, or extending a glad hand to, each set of newcomers. While each of the migratory influxes has followed certain patterns peculiar to itself, there has been a tone and a predictable sequence of rhetoric in one way or another common to them all; there has also been a classic pattern of "adaptation" or "assimilation." As they enter the city, the Puerto Ricans hear this same rhetoric, but whether they can follow the classic pattern of assimilation in the middle of the twentieth century is an open question.

I

The rhetoric of this latest migration reached its peak in the spring and summer of 1947, when, after war, spokesmen for various interests were duly fearful of a slump. Their rhetoric was a whispering echo of that which has been heard at various times throughout American history, especially during the second decade of the century, when the Americanization crusade was under way. It comes out of the same context of distrust and fear of strangers as the Nativist activities of the 1830's, the Know Nothing movement of the 1850's, the APA-ism of the 1890's, and the Ku Klux Klan rides of the 1920's.

The Puerto Ricans were seen by many spokesmen and commentators as a continuation of the "new immigration," from South and East Europe rather than of the "old immigration" from West and North Europe. Many of them are dark, even Negro; there is a rather high illiteracy rate among them; they are Catholic; although citizens, they lack training in full political participation; the island from which they come is economically backward.

Comments picked at random suffice to indicate the content of the press about Puerto Ricans. Two authors claim that they are "mostly crude farmers, subject to congenital tropical diseases . . . almost impossible to assimilate and condition . . . a majority of these people are lured here deliberately, because as American citizens they can vote . . . few can obtain employment . . . they were left far behind in their own unhappy land before they left, that was why they left . . . they turn to guile and wile and the steel blade, the traditional weapon of the sugar cane cutter, mark of their blood and heritage. . . ."[4] When the Commissioner of Welfare said there was a 54 per cent rise in the non-resident case load in a year due to Puerto Rican arrivals,[5] one newsman wrote: "New York City's relief costs have jumped 54 per cent in areas where Puerto Ricans congregate."[6] Three days later, the city was "reeling under the impact of this continuing immigration, suffering along with the migrants for all the dislocation caused by such an ill-advised, unsound shifting of the population."[7]

Another comment, which seems to come from recent newspaper clippings on the Puerto Ricans, actually was written about the Irish in 1840: "The conditions under which they had been born and brought up were generally of the most squalid and degrading character. Their wretched hovels, thatched with rotting straw, scantily furnished with light, hardly ventilated at all, frequently with no floor but the clay on which they were built, were crowded beyond the bounds of comfort, health, or, as it would seem to us, of simple social decency; their beds were heaps of straw or rags; their food consisted mainly of buttermilk and potatoes, often of the worst, and commonly inadequate in amount; their clothing was scanty and shabby."[8]

Always with each new wave there has been such a cry. "This time it is different"; perhaps "when the country was new it might have been good policy to admit all. But it is so no longer." That is what Representative Otis of Massachusetts told his colleagues in 1797.[9] Nor has this rhetoric been confined to newspapers or officials. As a whole, American historians of older stock have taken a belligerent attitude, declaring for the superiority of the "Anglo-Saxon," maintaining that the immigrant "somehow constituted a threat to what they held dear, ideologically and materially." On the other hand, "the jingoism of the historians of recent immigrant ancestry far exceeded the chauvinism of historians derived from the older American stock."[10]

Examining the record and the rhetoric, one cannot escape the conclusion that streets "filled with wandering crowds of immigrants . . . clustering in our cities, unacquainted with our climate, without employment, without friends, not speaking our language . . ." as the Mayor of New York City described them in 1837,[11] have been a large and continuous part of the American experience, and each time this rhetoric has accompanied it.

2

As successive waves of immigrants have swept into Manhattan and elsewhere in America, a rather clear-cut pattern of their experience and of the reactions of native Americans has been established. Most of the newcomers are poor, and hence forced into the least desirable sections of the city, from two to ten families often living in accommodations built for one. They are uneducated; the ways of the new city are strange and complex; the ways of yet another culture add to their strangeness and complexity; they are exploited by native landlords and sharks, and by some of their own countrymen who already "know the ropes." Entering the labor market, unlearned, unskilled, they seem at the mercy of economic forces. If the business cycle is on the upturn, they are welcomed; if it is on the way down, or in the middle of one of its periodic breakdowns, there is a savage struggle for even the low wage jobs between the new immigrants and the earlier ones who feel they have a prior claim.

The new group huddles together for comfort in mutual misery, and then is accused of "clannishness." Yet the immigrant group itself is almost never cohesive, but is crisscrossed by economic cleavages, inter-village rivalries, rural-urban lines, and sometimes by religious differences, educational rank, and vocation. But if the group as a whole has one visibly distinguishing characteristic, it is that all members are usually lumped together by the "natives"; whatever distinguishing tag is given the group is applied willy-nilly to each and every individual in it.

The press and the politicians usually take the lead in influencing public opinion about the newcomers. Foreigners make news, which by definition has to do with the unusual. The more their manners and morals differ, the more newsworthy they become. No matter how bad the slum conditions in which the children of older immigrant groups live, they are not considered newsworthy, but slum conditions in which the children of newcomers live make the front page. High crime rates of slum dwellers as such are not news, but a few crimes committed by the recent immigrants may constitute a "crime wave."[12] The conspicuous strangers become a convenient foil for attacks which give politicians publicity and the backing of the uneducated, the anxious nationalists, the professional patriots, and special interest groups.

The competition and conflict which mark the early years of former immigrant groups gradually give way to accommodation. Older established immigrant groups find that their economic and social status is not actually threatened by the newcomers; businessmen discover that the newcomers are among their customers; employers find that the strangers can do their work; unions find that language barriers can be overcome and that the immigrant in due course may become a loyal union member.

The new group itself begins to adapt to its new environment. English words and phrases begin to replace the mother tongue;[13] some of the newcomers go to night school and learn the new language, new customs, and new skills. The birth rate, originally high because of ignorance and poverty, begins to decline.[14] Finally the migrants begin a slow climb up the American occupational ladder. They establish businesses and churches, mutual aid associations and newspapers.[15] They become citizens. The politicians then find that they are not a "menace to America" after all, but actually are bringing, just as their predecessors did, elements of new life and strength to "the greatest nation in the world."

Having gained acceptance, the newcomers begin a process of "assimilation." They become active outside their own group and occupation, in various civic, business, religious, and labor organizations. They are welcomed at community affairs; they mix with the "old timers" on a more or less equal basis; they have "arrived."

This pattern is subject to local variation by the stratification of each different community, but in general it has been followed by all major immigrant groups since the first wave 300 years ago.

Community welfare and educational agencies play a crucial role in the reciprocal adaptation of the newcomers and the settled population. Education has presented touchy problems to both groups. Its *motif* has gradually changed from coercive attempts at wiping out foreign characteristics to an appreciation of the cultural contributions the newcomers can make. Some time has passed since it was possible to make the kind of statement issued by the Americanization superintendent of the New York Public Schools in 1918: "Broadly speaking, we mean (by Americanization) an appreciation of the institutions of this country and absolute forgetfulness of all obligations or connections with other countries because of descent or birth."[16] Yet in a world in a state of semicontinuous war, we may hear it again.

With the recent decline of immigration, cultural pluralism, a new approach to the solution of problems arising from the presence of divergent cultures, has been taken seriously by small circles of people. This perspective assumes the bankruptcy of the "melting pot" theory, asserting that to attack group values is likely to strengthen them. More importantly, it proposes that each cultural group may have something to contribute to American civilization as a mixed cultural whole. Cultural pluralism is, of course, part of the general liberal view of nationalism in America, which sees the future nation as a progressively happier and more tolerant integration of diverse cultural tendencies.

"If the cultural pluralism theory is correct," writes Dean E. George Payne, "then the problem of adjustment becomes essentially that of preserving cultural traits, of dignifying qualities and practices different from our own, and of creating a feeling of pride in the folkways, mores, customs, conventions, and social patterns, characteristic of the immigrant in his homeland as well as of the Negro and the Indian. Education, therefore, under this theory assumes a totally different role. It begins by discovering their characteristics, by magnifying them, by dignifying them, and by creating a feeling of pride in them."[17]

Thus, a new rhetoric has come about, but despite its acceptance by small groups of upper middle class professionals, whenever a new migratory group of any size and difference enters the city, the old rhetoric is taken out and refurbished.

3

Certainly the Puerto Ricans have heard the old, intolerant rhetoric of the middle forties, but whether they will follow the classic pattern of assimilation is a different question. Will they, as a group and as individuals, move gradually, or rapidly, or at all toward some kind of integration with the accepted patterns of New York life? Will their children begin the American climb away from the asperities their parents face into a white-collar job or a secure business?

The Puerto Ricans must be classed as part of "the new immigration," many of whose members have not followed the classic pattern with the ease some liberal commentators suppose, or, indeed, have not followed it at all.[18] Characteristics of the new setting of their migration must be borne in mind when attempting to forecast the possibilities for Puerto Ricans.

The islanders come at a time when the rate of upward mobility, a key feature of the classic pattern, has been slowing down. It is quite possible that again, as during the thirties, the ladder will become something of a treadmill. Between this migration and the migration before World War I stands the fact of the big slump. Before 1920, immigration into the United States aided, and was part of, the rapid expansion of the economy. Indisputably, what happens to a new immigration depends directly upon what happens to the economy. Immigration aside, will the economy continue to expand? Between 1870 and 1930, jobs increased 300 per cent, population 200 per cent.[19] But can this trend begin again?

Puerto Ricans in New York are twentieth-century migrants who have entered the economic framework of twentieth-century America; in particular, they are handworkers who enter a class structure that has become increasingly rigid since the end of the nineteenth century. They are identifiable in New York not only as the representatives of a "foreign culture," but as belonging to a specific economic position. As long as their sphere of experience is closed off by low status and lack of occupational diversity, the opportunity to become assimilated is likewise restricted.

In the city, Puerto Ricans are concentrated in unskilled and semiskilled jobs, mainly in manufacturing and service industries. They are most likely to remain at the skill level at which they enter the New York labor market. Those who do move upward occupationally meet a ceiling at the handwork level. They may rise from unskilled to semiskilled or even to skilled levels, but white-collar work or small business, to which, in the classic pattern they should aspire, is largely closed to them.

The handwork jobs available to the migrants, and the industries in which they are employed, are just those most subject to business fluctuations. Escape from this sort of lower-level working class lies, as the Puerto Rican sees it, mainly in the small business field. In Harlem, for example, many retail grocery stores and other small businesses are owned by Puerto Ricans. Eight years ago a Negro writer, describing conditions in Harlem, reported that, "Today 99 per cent of the community's commerce is done by Puerto Ricans and other members of the Spanish-speaking colonies."[20] Yet these are the very types of business which have the highest mortality.[21]

The "average Puerto Rican," then, can expect to have a harder time following the classic upward pattern in New York City than the European migrant of a generation past. Of course, "the average Puerto Rican" is a statistical abstraction. In any given group there are always individual variations, and it is true that "the Puerto Ricans," like all others are split into many subclasses. There are many older groups of migrants from earlier, small migrations who have already made good, who own grocery stores, small stands, and other businesses. A few Puerto Rican migrants are famous and successful—José Ferrer, the actor and director, Jesús María Sanromá, the pianist, Graciela Rivera, coloratura soprana, Noro Morales, composer and orchestra leader, Luis Juero Chiesa, artist and illustrator of children's books. Such variations, however, do not deny the validity of the general sociological type and its typical problems.

4

Yet one reality of United States culture denies that the Puerto Rican is one single type: the Puerto Ricans differ from previous migrants to this country in that a third of them are Negroes. They are the only substantial influx of colored migrants from a non-English speaking culture which New York has known. The world into which they move when they come to the city is largely a Negro world, with all the restrictions imposed upon it by a white society. They enter this country, as migrants, at a time when opportunities for the entire group are by no means large, and when other tensions about them are by no means low. Movement upward in the American social scene for them is not only circumscribed as it is for all immigrants, but also by the ceilings which United States culture places upon the aspirations of all Negroes in America.

But there is a curious contradiction within American society which gives higher status to the foreign-born Negro, and particularly the non-English-speaking Negro, than to the native American Negro. Of necessity, the colored Puerto Rican is encouraged to maintain his identity as a "foreigner" rather than to blend himself in the world of the American Negro. Especially is this true for those in the intermediate colored group, the grifos, whose Caucasian features entitle them to a somewhat higher status on the island than the outright Negro or mulatto, but who in New York may lose that margin of privilege.

These colored Puerto Ricans have less incentive and less opportunity to follow the pattern of Americanization than any other immigrants America has known. Only so long as they continue to remain conspicuously different from the American Negro can they improve their status in America.

5

There is still another important respect in which the Puerto Rican migration differs from nineteenth- and early twentieth-century migrations: it is in larger part a migration of women.

Up to 1930, most immigrants to the United States were men who, once they managed to make their way, sent for their wives and families. In the decade, 1901–10, only 30.2 per cent of the migrants to the United States were women; in 1921–30, 44.4 per cent. Since the twenties, however, immigration figures have shown increasing proportions of women entering the country; during the thirties, 56.6 per cent of the immigrants were women; in the last half of the forties, 59.0 per cent.[22]

Yet, there is a basic difference between the overseas immigrants and the island migrants in this respect. For the most part, women from Europe have been those who could legally join relatives who had entered this country before the immigration laws. In the late twenties and during the thirties, therefore, immigrant women were those who joined husbands, balancing a sex ratio that had previously been overwhelmingly male. Even though the official entry figures show a higher proportion of women, once they entered their ethnic groups in the United States, the statistical ratio disappeared. This is not the case in the Puerto Rican colonies. Since its beginning in the twenties, the Puerto Rican migration has consistently shown a preponderance of women. In New York they outnumber the men about three to two. Among the non-white migrants this preponderance of women is even more marked.[23]

Many women who leave the island for New York do come to join their families, but there is also a large number of single girls and women who have been divorced, deserted, or widowed. For them, the city becomes a place of new freedom—a place where they can be free of the restrictions Latin culture would place upon them. But their comparative inexperience with an unsupervised life sometimes brings them into conspicuous public view; and here again newspaper assertions about the "loose morals" and the high prostitution rate of the Puerto Rican colony feed the rhetoric of migration. The courting behavior of any women migrants is always particularly dramatic to observers outside the migrant community if it differs in any way from

American custom; it feeds the press and rhetoricians, supports and releases other hostilities from the surrounding communities.

The colored women, particularly the intermediately colored, have an even more acute problem. As New York's colonies contain about twice as many of these women as men, the women are forced to seek male companionship outside the Puerto Rican colony, perhaps even outside their color group. The range of their social circulation is defined by mainland standards as the sphere reserved for the American Negro. Yet in the due course of exposure to American prejudice, the colored Puerto Rican woman, especially if grifo or indio, is likely to consider American Negroes beneath her social status. But if she crosses into the white community she is acting conspicuously, focusing mainland attention upon her noticeably "different" behavior.

That the Puerto Rican migration is preponderantly made up of women also affects the way in which and the degree to which migrant colonists become adjusted to continental life. Adjustment to a culture requires the exposure of new members to older ones; association at work is a direct means of such exposure. Although many of the Puerto Rican women do have jobs, there is still a substantial proportion who are housewives. The circulation of these women, like that of all Latin women, is more restricted than that of men. Moreover, the geographical area of their activities is more circumscribed; they confine themselves mainly to the household, the street, and the neighborhood.

While presumably the women who work have a better opportunity to "learn the ropes" in the New York world, actually they are confined to highly limited occupations and industries. Even more than the men they are restricted to semiskilled jobs in manufacturing industries. Thus, although working women have more of a chance than housewives to be exposed to American culture, their chance is limited to a small sector of it. The virtual absence of job mobility among Puerto Rican women seems to deny the likelihood of future change in these conditions.

There is another respect in which the preponderance of women among the migrants seems to affect their chances of adjustment. One of the strongest incentives to adaptation among immigrants is their wish for job advancement. But, unlike the men, the women are likely to view their jobs mainly as a supplementary source of money in the family. They are much less career-minded than the men; Spanish culture does not encourage women to aspire upward occupationally. To them, "job advancement" is more likely to mean either the opportunity to earn more money for the same work, or to leave the labor market entirely to become housewives.

In summary, movement of the Puerto Ricans according to the classic pattern of assimilation is slowed up or hampered by (1) the facts that the Puerto Ricans—men and women, white and colored—are occupationally restricted, and that they enter a social order with a declining rate of upward mobility, so that they have less chance than previous migrants to be exposed to American culture while on the way up; (2) the fact that two thirds of the migrants are, by mainland standards, colored, and thus cannot rise as easily or as far as people of white stock, and may thus presumably develop less motivation to fit themselves into the lower levels of a world of color and caste; (3) the fact that among the migrants there are more women than men, and that women have less opportunity to become exposed to any culture outside their households, the housewives among them because their range of social circulation is so limited, the working women because they are, and are likely to remain, concentrated occupationally.

6. *The Puerto Rican World*

TRAVELING the geographical distance from Puerto Rico to New York City is the least part of the migrant's journey. To find even minimal comfort in the city he must cross an enormous cultural and social distance, to a world that presents more contrasts than similarities to the world he knew.

In Puerto Rico, 70 per cent of the people live in the open country or in small villages,[1] and even though the migrant is already a city dweller, a Puerto Rican city is not like New York. The larger framework of island life is that of scattered farms, a point, incidentally, in which Puerto Rico differs from most Latin American republics, where village clusters are almost universal. In this rural society, the economic and the family unit coincide; social relations are largely intimate and face to face; community controls are strong, at times even oppressive; time is measured by the position of the sun; sanitation is rudimentary—hogs and goats eat the garbage thrown into the yards, and the sun and rain neutralize excrement.

In New York, world center and quintessence of urbanism, families are small and are no longer economic units of production; social contacts are transitory and impersonal; community controls have given way to a more distant institutional framework; the individual is anonymous; time is measured by the second hand of the watch; sanitation is a minutely organized and expensive machinery of big grey trucks.

In the Puerto Rican city one still lives in a recognizable and structured community; the plaza still forms the center of social life. Here one strolls during the evening to find friends and neighbors whose history everyone knows, whose family everyone can identify for generations back. On the stone benches flirtations, engagements, marriages are arranged and discussed. One knows one's neighbor, and exchanges the social amenities. In the apartments and the houses, windows are always open, doors are seldom locked.

However split the island community may be, however many contradictions may run through it, life there is still intertwined with knowable and consistent themes: it is a community. In the metropolis the migrant has no community, even in the clusters of Puerto Rican settlement. Now the center of social organization is at best a household, which is itself subject to strong tendencies toward fragmentation into homeless and anxiety-ridden individualism. Any attempts the migrant might make to enlarge his world outside the household are beset by great difficulties and seemingly endless frustration. In so far as he is socially regulated in soft, informal ways, it is by his household and close-up neighbors; beyond that the organizations that regulate him are not of his own creation. He is in a world he never made.

I

Physically, a migrant household contrasts sharply with an island home.

In Puerto Rico, where the weather is warm and sunny, housing may be reduced to the barest essentials. The poorest man in the country may secure for himself a few boards, or the hard dry leaves of a palm tree, and patch up a small *bohío*, or hut. The bushes around the house afford any necessary privacy. Those who have greater economic security and more education have more comfortable houses, of course, and there are mansions with all modern conveniences.

The range and contrast in housing on the island is narrower than in New York. On the island median monthly rentals in 1940 were about $4, and only 87 families paid more than $100 monthly. In New York City, although the median rental was about $38 in 1940, the record top was $18,000 a year for a

33-room apartment. This would have paid the total annual rent bill in some Puerto Rican villages. Only 0.3 per cent of the island homes were worth $10,000 or more, and 61 per cent were valued at less than $100 in 1940, but single neighborhoods in New York contain many families each of which spends $10,000 or more per year.[2]

There was no running water in over three quarters of the Puerto Rican island dwelling units in 1940; no toilet or privy in over one fourth; only 29 per cent had electricity.[3] A Puerto Rican apartment in New York is likely to contain these improvements, even though they may be in bad repair.

Yet on United States standards, the housing available to the Puerto Ricans in Manhattan and the Bronx is uniformly poor. Because of their relatively low salaries, only the cheapest dwellings are available to them. Dwelling units in Manhattan are less adequate, smaller, more crowded, and in poorer repair than those in the Bronx. A recent study of a Puerto Rican block in Manhattan states that "landlords do not make repairs. . . . Tenants are afraid to report violations, even serious ones, because upon official inspection the whole house may be condemned. If a building is condemned, the Housing Authority must rehouse the tenants, and this the Authority cannot do because there are no vacancies. . . . The result is continuous deterioration of houses and lowering of living conditions."[4] Our interviewers often reported spotlessly clean apartments crawling with roaches, the housewife frantic and frustrated. Leaking roofs ("We have to wear rubbers when it rains"), broken windows, and splintered steps are common. "The alleyways and streets are filthy, the garbage man never comes this way." Frequently, the Puerto Rican family must bribe the superintendent or agent in order to obtain even the worst apartment.

Yet dwellings in New York's Puerto Rican colonies do offer improved means of life; for example, refrigeration is highly available in New York: in San Juan 74 per cent of the dwelling units were without any refrigeration in 1940, while in Puerto Rican settlements of Manhattan and the Bronx, only 14 per cent of the dwelling units were without iceboxes or refrigerators.[5]

On the average, the Puerto Rican household in New York is only slightly smaller (4.4 persons) than the island household (4.8 persons), and practically the same as the San Juan (4.3 persons). There are fewer "crowded households" in New York's Puerto Rican colonies than on the island: 43 per cent of the households in New York, and 55 per cent in Puerto Rico, contain five or more residents.

The New York migrant's household often contains an extended family: relatives other than the immediate conjugal unit (33 per cent), or "boarders" (16 per cent) live in half the households studied; the other half (51 per cent) of the households consist of husband, wife, and their children. This may in part be due to the housing shortage, during which so many New York families have had to double up; but it also fits the extended family pattern of the island.

Press photos of ten or fifteen persons huddled in one small apartment do not reveal typical cases. Families do live under such crowded conditions, but they are unusual. The average Puerto Rican family in either of New York's two core areas has an apartment of 4.2 rooms, a median density of 1.2 persons per room in Manhattan and 1.3 persons per room in the Bronx area. They are somewhat more crowded than the general population in these boroughs, where average room density, according to the 1940 census, was a little under one person per room. But housing conditions have changed so much since 1940 that such a comparison can scarcely be considered reliable.

Generally, members of the Puerto Rican household in New York pool earnings in a common purse. When money from all sources is considered, the median income per family is $36.28 per week; two thirds of the families receive less than $40. Migrants in Manhattan are slightly worse off than those in the Bronx; 20 per cent in the Bronx but 31 per cent in Manhattan earn under $30 a week. These differences represent in part the lower earning capacity of the colored migrants who cluster in Manhattan.

Per capita income is higher for the smaller than the larger households, since the larger the unit, the more children or old people beyond working age there are in proportion to the number of earners. The median per capita income, from all sources, of Puerto Ricans in the core areas is $14.46. On all these objective economic counts, the migrants' households are somewhat better off than the islanders', but not as well off as the general New York population.

2

The family is the basic set of relations of the Puerto Rican migrant in New York City. A Puerto Rican "family" is defined by residence rather than blood. All those who live together in the same apartment and share its expenses—immediate and extended kin, ritual kin, and friends from the home town— regard each other as "living in the family," whether related by blood or not. Of course, such standard relations as father-mother- child and husband-wife still form the core of the social unit. Sharing an apartment creates a sense of belonging and of unity; the Spanish familiar "tu" is almost universal.

These members of the household are often related by the migration pattern itself. As we have noted,[6] it is usually the most economically able individual—the father or the oldest son or daughter—who is the first to migrate. This "first migrant" often stays with a relative or friend from Puerto Rico, and, as soon as he is able, sends for other members of the family and sets up a new household unit, of which he becomes the head. Neighbors, relatives, and friends in Puerto Rico are stimulated to come by the migrant already in New York, or they themselves suggest that the prior migrant help them by providing a room, and on many occasions, a job.

The division of labor inside the household is generally defined by sex and age, although it is complicated by priorities of mi- gration and by work outside the house. All adult members of the family are expected to work and to contribute to the support of the house in some way. The mother or daughter, who works or goes to school, cooks supper, a common family meal; and all the women are expected to help in cleaning, washing, and general household work. Typically, men are not expected to help in the recently arrived migrant households, but their duties in household work sometimes increase as they are in New York longer. Among the recently arrived, the Puerto Rican idea that housework is a woman's job still prevails. Here the new adaptation is apparently not learned directly from contact with non-"Latin" men, but is more connected with the fact that women go out to work.

In Puerto Rico the wife who did work typically did so in the home, contributing only a small sum to the family income; in New York, as we have seen, many women work, at least for a time, and often make considerable income by Puerto Rican standards. In New York there are greater opportunities for women to work, and the economic situation more frequently prompts them to do so. The husband, who generally in Puerto Rico was opposed to his wife's working away from home, is now more willing to accept it. He is also more willing to live off her income than he would have been in Puerto Rico, where it would have been a cause for shame. The practice of homework in a farmed-out system, such as sewing, is rarer in New York, so that the woman finds a greater amount of freedom in her goings and comings which in Puerto Rico were limited strictly to necessary purchases and, possibly, going to church. She acquires some feeling of independence while she is working, though nothing like the independence of the continental woman.

Among the more recently arrived migrants, the husband is the head of the house, and the wife may even feel that in his absence she should show a mask of ignorance and fear before strangers. Newcomers, of either sex, may say they should not speak because they are not the "owners of the house." Yet women who do not have a steady husband but who pay the rent are regarded as "owners," and are the authority in the house. Authority is apparently connected to this single item of paying the house rent, except with women who married their husbands in Puerto Rico.

That Puerto Rican women may be cash-providers has made their position higher in the city. The belief that women are "more protected" by such formal institutions as the police and the courts, etc. contributes to this lift in status, and its acceptance by Puerto Rican men. The effects of their new position, especially among the married women or those who have a permanent sex relationship with a man, modify the general pattern of man-woman relations. Such a woman may even share authority with her husband, vote differently from him, have a different religion, and often have her beliefs and opinions respected by her husband.

Many women in the new situation revolt against the accepted island pattern of male dominance. One woman, interviewed while working at a semiskilled job, expressed the point as follows: "Whether I have a husband or not I work. So I do what I want, and if my husband dare to complain, I throw him out. That is the difference; in Puerto Rico I should have to stand for anything a man asks me to do because he pays the rent. Here I belong to myself." The male reaction is typified by these words: "Women get lost with the liberty they have up here and many, not all, become bitches." Unmarried women migrants, more frequently than married women, are regarded as "demoralized" by virtue of their new independence. If the husband begins to earn a sufficient amount to support his family, the wife will in all probability stop working. Then her feeling of being tied down will be even greater, not only because she has experienced a little freedom, but because here, as compared with Puerto Rico, there is usually little opportunity for contact with people outside her own apartment building. She does not know most of her neighbors and often may feel very much closed-in. Her situation may be further complicated by the following attitude:

Interviewer: "What are your favorite amusements?"
Respondent: "I go to the movies often and to dances and to bars for a drink."
Interviewer: "Do you take your wife along?"

Respondent: "No, wherever I go I go alone. She is supposed to
stay at home. She knows that if she doesn't please me
I can send her away and take another in her place—
that is why she tries to be a good wife because she
loves me very much and wants to be with me. I love
her too, but that doesn't mean that I can't go out
with other women while she is at home."

Changes in parent-child relations in the New York household
are connected with the belief that here children, like women, are
"protected by the government" and a generally higher status is
consequently granted to them. This belief may even go to the
point of defining children as being under government care and
responsibility. The effects of this changing relation are apparently
a source of conflict for many Puerto Rican parents in the city.
Fearing what the government might do, the Puerto Rican parent
may decline to control his child. The immediate results are ver-
balized by parents thus: "Children here grow up as bandits, they
cannot be scolded or punished," "A child takes you to court if
you beat him," "The judge believes more to a child than to you,"
"Children need control. They are too free here and one is for-
bidden to punish them." And another said: "Children are not
taught to respect older people, as they are in Puerto Rico." Apparently, therefore, children are allowed to do what they want.
At any rate, the opinions of children are heard and considered
by parents even on issues connected with such matters as their
sex life.

Difficulties often arise when children learn English and find
that they hold a whip hand over the parents who speak only
Spanish, or speak English brokenly. Sometimes the English-
speaking older child can get a job when the Spanish-speaking
father cannot. This kind of experience, if repeated day after day,
contributes greatly to an insecure second generation. The children are estranged from the parents and their culture and from
the neighbors and theirs. They become the culturally homeless,
to whom not social, but institutional, controls are applicable. The
Puerto Rican family, in the lower classes a rather loose-jointed

affair, in New York City is subjected to further strain of a sort typical of immigrant groups. Yet it is still the center of the New York migrants' social world.

3

The world of the Puerto Rican migrant spreads out from family and household to include the apartment house or tenement in which the Puerto Rican lives. Relations within the apartment house are often very close, especially among people from the same home town but including any Puerto Rican in the building. Relatives—blood and ritual kin—in other buildings in the neighborhood are also within this network. These are the people who probably visit each other more or less regularly and in a casual and informal way; in fact such visiting among Puerto Ricans outside of the immediate areas seems to be rare. Like the Polish immigrant colony, the Puerto Rican migrants' world is primarily the "Okolica," the "neighborhood round . . . as far as a man is talked about."[7] Italians in the Battery, at least 25 years ago, settled in a pattern whose ecological units here were set up according to villages and even streets of Italy and Sicily.[8] There is some evidence that the household and friendship patterns among the Puerto Ricans often have a similar locality basis.

Relations with other Puerto Ricans outside the apartment house tend to be insecure and casual, with only a few exceptions: in the East Harlem area, groups of Puerto Rican men meet in the restaurants and bars to chat, notwithstanding the hour of the day or the night. The travel agency also seems to have become a center for informal meetings of Puerto Ricans. Women often gather at grocery stores and the Park Avenue market place in East Harlem.

In slum areas, poor housing drives social life into the street. To the Puerto Rican this is a familiar pattern, but in New York, instead of communities in the sun, there is only congregation in the cold. New York streets, crowded, often cold and dirty, always hurried, offer a poor substitute for the community interaction that existed in the slower pace and more ample life of the

Puerto Rican plaza. At best they offer only corners on which to cluster, candy stores, strident bars, or narrow cafés where in order to stay one must buy. Street communities, as everywhere in New York, produce "drugstore cowboys" and street gangs. Many of our respondents reported trouble on their streets.

Beyond the household, the apartment house, and the street, lies greater New York City, where everything seems more complex and more distant than the islander is accustomed to. Density of population is a familiar phenomenon to the migrant since his island is one of the most densely populated places in the world (640 persons per square mile), yet he is quite unprepared for the 86,000 persons per square mile on Manhattan.[9]

In Puerto Rico the distances from one place to another are relatively short; after all, the entire island is not as large as the state of Connecticut. The longest journey, from one shore to the other, takes no more than a day by car or bus, but such a trip is regarded as a relatively serious undertaking. If the migrant was a skilled worker in Puerto Rico, he probably took a short bus ride or walk to a small shop consisting of no more than 50 to 100 workers. If he gets a job in a New York factory, however, he must roar on the juggernaut of the subway to a plant with hundreds or even thousands of workers. The relatively informal pace of work that he knew in Puerto Rico is replaced by the rigid time structure of the modern factory.

Along with the gulf of cultural distance and pace, these factors of time and place must be surmounted by the Puerto Rican who attempts to enlarge his world beyond tenement and street. He makes such an attempt in various ways, among them, friendships and organizations, including welfare agencies, and the formal media of communication.

4

When a Puerto Rican migrates, he either requests or is offered help from relatives or friends in finding a job and a place to live. The world he enters is not only a general Puerto Rican milieu, but specifically that of his former locality. If he knows others from his home town, and usually he does, he feels something in common with them. Even if they are no longer his neighbors, he tends to seek them out for the alleviation of nostalgia and home-sickness, for the informal security, each provides the other. Cliques develop from these assumed ties, their strength being in rough inverse proportion to the range of the migrants' other contacts.

Holiday sentiment strengthens and facilitates, as well as pro-vides an outlet for this localism, which may be the base from which Puerto Rican nationalism in New York develops. One of our observers reports, "I met a Puerto Rican man in the street and told him I would like him to tell me about the Puerto Ricans in New York City. He said: 'Come with me to the Bronx and I'll show you how after all the years in the States we keep our customs alive.' I asked him if he had anything particular in mind and he replied: 'Today is the last day of Christmas, it is the Three Kings Day. My wife and I are expecting a gang from Utuado coming to play the guitar, cuatro, guicharo, and the maracas. The neighbors probably are coming as soon as they hear the music.'"

In New York, friendship does not seem greatly to enlarge the social world of the migrants beyond the household, for the house-hold becomes the center for most friendships: 64 per cent of the men, and 83 per cent of the women, say they usually meet their friends in their homes. Women are less likely than men to have social meetings in public places or at work. Only 8 per cent of the women, but 19 per cent of the men report that they use pub-lic places—stores and shops, streets, restaurants, bars, dance halls, clubs—for meeting with friends. Fifteen per cent of the men, and 6 per cent of the women, frequently meet friends at work. Only 2 or 3 per cent of either sex meet them in church.

One way to judge how well a person is getting along in his social world and how ample that world is, has to do with the numbers of "real" friends he has. We asked a set of questions clustered around friendships, leading off with: "Do you have any real friends in New York?" and, if yes, "About how many?"

Fifteen per cent answered that they had a great many "real" friends in New York, 61 per cent said they had only a few, and 24 per cent said they had none.

Men are more apt to have more friends than women, women being more restricted to the household and hence having less opportunity to make friends. And, among both men and women, the early arrivals have only a few more friends than those who came to New York later, even though they have had more time in which either to make friends or bring their friends to New York from Puerto Rico. There are no consistent variations according to race.

When asked where it was more difficult to *make* "real" friends —in New York or Puerto Rico—58 per cent of the respondents said it was more difficult in New York, while 40 per cent said that it was the same in both places; only 2 per cent said that it was more difficult in Puerto Rico. More of the recent than of the earlier migrants find it more difficult to have real friends in New York than in Puerto Rico; and among the newcomers, women are slightly more apt to express difficulties than men.

Similarly, over one half (56 per cent) of the migrants declare that they find it more difficult to *meet with* friends in New York than on the island. Recent women migrants have the most difficulty (65 per cent); early men migrants have the least (24 per cent). Time of arrival is less important among women than men, probably because, even after they have been here a while, the women venture less from their homes. Thus, unless a woman's friends live nearby or in the same apartment house she finds it difficult to get out to meet them. There are no significant constant racial differences; but of all groups, white men who have been here a long time meet friends easiest, only 10 per cent of them say that they have more difficulty in New York than in Puerto Rico.

When the migrants are asked to explain why they think it is more difficult to *meet* with friends in New York, their answers refer predominantly to the changed pace of life. The change from island to city is not only a change of cultural milieu, but also of the entire tempo of the migrant's life, even if he comes from an island city.

On the island, dividing the day into morning, afternoon, and evening is ordinarily sufficient. Hours, minutes, and seconds become important only in a more highly developed and more intricately organized industrial civilization. The islander's comfortable attitude that a task can wait until "mañana" is assaulted by the huge sign on the shop wall, "DO IT NOW." The sophisticated Puerto Rican on the island, fixing an hour of meeting with a continental friend, may ask, "Do you mean 5 o'clock Puerto Rican or American time?"

TABLE VI-1. WHY IS IT MORE DIFFICULT IN NEW YORK...
TO MEET WITH FRIENDS...AND TO MAKE REAL
FRIENDS...THAN IN PUERTO RICO?

Reasons	More difficult to meet with friends	More difficult to make "real" friends
Urban Life	91%	46%
Time	55	32
Distance; travel	36	14
Changed Culture	23%	65%
Changed customs	4	7
People in New York	8	24
You know people better in Puerto Rico	—	21
Language	2	3
Other	9%	10%
TOTAL[a]	(606)	(548)

[a] The percentages add to more than 100 since some respondents gave more than one reason.

When the islander comes to the metropolis, he works longer hours, and more days in a week. His shop is far from his home. Everywhere everyone is rushing. Ninety-one per cent of the sample report that urban time and distance seriously cut into their meetings with friends, whereas only 23 per cent speak in terms of the difficulties created by the changed culture. Considering that one of the main "pulls" New York exercises upon migrants is precisely the existence of the Puerto Rican community in the city, this is not surprising.

When asked to explain why it is more difficult to *make* "real" friends in New York, some migrants still referred to the heightened pace of New York life, but the proportion drops from 91 to 46 per cent.

For making new friends, the migrants find that it is the changed culture which presents the greater difficulty. Two thirds of the sample explain that it is harder to get to make "real" friends because people and customs are different in New York. People in New York are "outright unpleasant," say 24 per cent. "They are not the kind you want for real friends!" "They are peculiar; they don't know the meaning of friendship." Another 21 per cent do not feel as strongly: "In New York you don't get to know people very well, the way you did in Puerto Rico," they say, without referring to specific unpleasant characteristics. Ten per cent refer to the language barrier, or changed customs and ways of doing things in New York.

The migrant's race is most important in affecting his sensitivity to New York's changed culture. And it is the intermediately colored Puerto Ricans, both men and women, rather than the white or Negro, who find the changed culture of New York most clearly a barrier to friendships. About one half of the white and colored men, but fully two thirds of the intermediate men declared that they found people in New York and their customs peculiar. Among women, 57 per cent of the "light" women, as compared with 46 per cent of Negro and white, mention changed culture.

Most Puerto Rican migrants know at least some people in New York whom they consider "real" friends, and more as they are here longer, but it is harder in New York for them to meet with their friends and to make "real" friends, than it was in Puerto Rico. Over half of all the groups, except the white men, continue to find friendships more difficult in New York; they feel differently, less warm and more suspicious, about the people they meet in New York.

5

The worlds of previous migrants to New York have often been created and enlarged by organizations of compatriots. The newly arrived immigrant joins a group whose members include older arrivals to the new country, who "show him the ropes," and thus soften the impact of his journey. Particularly has this been true of immigrants who come from cultures where organizations are central to the pattern of life. The Puerto Ricans have no such organizational tradition, and no "organized" Puerto Rican community seems to exist in New York City.

Such Puerto Rican organizations as do exist are few and weak. A newspaper campaign in 1947 brought to head an attempt to form a "united front" of all the scattered Puerto Rican groups, but it does not seem to have prospered. The few who do belong to groups do not tend to belong to strictly Puerto Rican or Latin organizations. Only 108 out of the 1113 migrants belong to general organizations; only 6 per cent of all the migrants belong to organizations which could be called Puerto Rican.

Organization members are more likely to be men: 13 per cent of the men as against 7 per cent of the women. Among both sexes, earlier arrivals are more apt to belong to organizations, but there are differences in the type of organizations to which they belong after they have been in New York awhile.

The longer the men are in the city, the more apt they are to belong to general organizations, the less likely to strictly Puerto Rican. But as the women are in the city longer they seem to turn more toward Puerto Rican organizations, and do not increase their 2 per cent membership in general organizations. But the important fact is that even among the early arrivals, 84 per cent of the men and 91 per cent of the women do not join organized groups.

TABLE VI-2. ORGANIZATION MEMBERSHIP OF THE MIGRANTS,
BY SEX AND TIME OF ARRIVAL

Organization membership	Men		Women	
	Recent	Early	Recent	Early
Belong to organizations	12%	16%	5%	9%
General	5	10	2	2
Puerto Rican	7	6	3	7
Belong to no organizations	88%	84%	95%	91%
TOTAL (100%)	(196)	(221)	(297)	(399)

One reason for the lack of organized groups is that "successful migrants" who might otherwise provide leadership usually move out of the core areas and lose their "Puerto Ricanness." They perfect their English, have steady jobs or businesses, fair or good incomes; they have made a more or less satisfactory adjustment. Generally those who have escaped from poverty are not interested in the plight of those who have not. "Many Puerto Ricans in New York refuse to identify themselves with the Harlem group in any way. The upper-class Latin-American, whether he be from Puerto Rico, Colombia, or any of the Latin-American countries, refers to the Harlem settlement as one of 'working people.'"[10] Thus, in addition to the racial cleavage of the group, to the extent that certain Puerto Ricans are "assimilated," there is a class split among the New York Puerto Ricans which is becoming more pronounced.

Indication of feelings about class differences appears in the belief among many migrants that "rich Puerto Ricans" make bad employers, paying very low wages. This refers particularly to domestic service. Puerto Rican social workers, who are apparently identified with the rich, or at any rate with a higher class, are sometimes said to be unfair to the Puerto Ricans whom they are supposed to help. Class feelings are carried over from Puerto Rico where there is quite widespread antagonism toward "the upper classes." The rich are often blamed for Puerto Rican conditions, and the upper class is generally identified as "the few rich people who refuse to invest their money in anything but sugar cane," and prevent the development of industries that would raise the standard of living and enable Puerto Ricans to remain on the island.

In the core settlements there seems to be little knowledge about where the better-off Puerto Ricans live, or even if they are concentrated in any particular place. Yet the antagonism can be picked up on the street, as in this example:

Near a newstand in East Harlem, an observer began to question a Negro woman, who replied: "I wish my husband be here. Because he knows of these things. Pass some other time, when he is around and he will tell you lots of things. He will tell you all the newspapers have said against us, and all because of A's fault. He started the campaign." "Who is A?" "A Puerto Rican who owns a B shop in C Street. He sends leaflets around the barrio insulting us. Of course, that is how the *World-Telegram* started, if one of us gave them the hand. And there was his picture in the newspapers! Rascal! He is a bad man. Too much money."

A man who came to buy a newspaper said: "That bastard he made his money bootlegging, everybody knows that. That is why he is a millionaire now. He has cars and everything so he goes on discrediting us. Don't mention me that man." And he walked away.

The woman continued: "A girl from the Bronx answered a good letter to the newspapers, she said she had the right to be here because her brother had fought for the United States in this war. If all the vets say the same thing the *Telegram* will shut its mouth. Come and talk to my husband." "When is he around?" "I don't know, he is in sometimes in the morning, and sometimes in the noon. It is like that, the poors have to do different things to live."

Several organizations do exist in the city among people connected by having the same home town in Puerto Rico, the same occupation in New York, or some such link. Some of the clubs have been in operation for over twenty years. The Puerto Rican, in fact, may not become interested in organizations until after a certain period of residence in the city, when in his acculturation process he becomes aware of the need of strengthening his links with Puerto Rico via a home town or other insular club. On the other hand, the clubs are often "American" in type. The patterns of trust among those who came to New York in more or less the same period, and the reverse, distrust of those who came later, probably help to explain the mutual lack of interest between the recent migrants and the older organizations. Only 2 per cent of our sample see their friends at club or organization meetings. The household is the important locale of Puerto Rican friendship: two thirds of the men and 80 per cent of the women say that they see their friends in their own homes. It is clear that organizations of Puerto Rican character do not play any key role in the life of the migrant.

Less than half of the Puerto Ricans have at any time taken advantage of their voting privileges in the city. White men vote more than any other group, and among the new arrivals, of course, the proportion who have never voted in New York City is higher than among the older residents. In view of the highly politicalized atmosphere of the island, the recent migrant's tendency to refrain from political activity in New York deserves discussion. Some 71 per cent of the eligible voters exercised their vote in the island in 1948, whereas 45 per cent did so on the continent. "On the island you grow up with the political issues," said one recent migrant. "They are part of your life. In New York, I don't even know who the candidates are, or what they are arguing about." And another: "When there is an election in New York, everything is quiet and you would hardly know it. No bands, no excitement, no parades. In Puerto Rico an election is a feast day."

Yet as the Puerto Ricans become more settled residents they are drawn into political participation. In the absence of any community organizations of their own "to help them when they are in trouble," and "to defend them in public," the machine of Congressman Vito Marcantonio functions. This machine, carried on in the personal manner of the old-style boss, has been highly successful in filling the lack of facilities among and for the migrants. As we shall presently see, Puerto Ricans are conditioned by their insular background not to turn to a public agency, but to seek help from a friend. If they do turn to a private or public agency, they may find no one on the staff who speaks Spanish. At the Marcantonio organization a friendly Spanish-speaking personnel is on hand to help the migrant. And, for favors received, what is more natural than a vote for a proved friend? Yet there is no correlation between voting and relief status, when time of arrival is properly controlled.[11] However, Mr. Marcantonio follows Puerto Rican affairs closely and is sometimes spoken of as the island's only Congressman. He has introduced bills providing for Puerto Rican independence and championed what many feel to be the island's interests in a number of respects. There is probably more sentiment for independence among the Puerto Ricans in New York than on the island where, in the recent election, only 10 per cent of the voters supported that program.

Mr. Marcantonio's influence, obviously, is not adversely affected by constant newspaper criticism of his friendship for the migrant. It seems likely to continue to flourish until other community organizations competitively succeed in servicing the needs of the migrants.

There is one type of organization to which the Puerto Ricans belong in imposing proportions: the labor unions. They already know something about unions from those on the island. The work they find in New York is usually in highly organized industries, and many become eligible for union membership. Several locals of the International Ladies Garment Workers Union are predominantly Puerto Rican; during the past several years Puerto Rican membership has increased in the Hotel and

Restaurant Workers Union; Puerto Ricans have been members of the National Maritime Union for many years; many are members of the Toy and Novelty workers unions.

Regardless of sex, color, or level of skill, Puerto Rican workers in New York are quite well organized: no less than 51 per cent of those now in the labor force report union membership. As the period of their residence in the city lengthens, there is no discernible tendency for more men to join unions, possibly because high proportions join at the beginning: 56 per cent of the recently arrived, 58 per cent of the older residents. Among women, however, the longer they are here, the more likely they are to be union members; 39 per cent of the recent, and 47 per cent of the earlier arrivals are unionized.

6

Fifty years of rule by a Protestant land have made no great inroads on the Puerto Ricans' formal adherence to the Catholic faith. About 85 per cent of the island population are Catholic. Although Protestant missions on the island have made a certain number of converts, and in New York City the Puerto Rican Protestant church is a growing institution, about 83 per cent of all the migrants in New York declared that they were Catholic, 9 per cent that they were Protestant. Five per cent belong to various other sects, and there is a thin stratum—about 2 per cent—of Spiritualists. Some social workers have reported what seems to them a high incidence of conversion hysteria among the migrants, especially women. Such expressions, once "accepted" in our own culture, are fairly common on the island; wives have "ataques" as a result of disputes with husbands, relatives, or friends. Certain individuals are treated tenderly because they are "nervous." The fairly numerous adherents of spiritualism may treat such hysterical attacks as a "possession" by some spirit.

Many Catholic Puerto Ricans who visit New York's colonies report that they are shocked at the casual way in which religious observances are performed in New York. For example, one respondent reported, "During Holy Week people eat meat, sing, and dance as if they were not aware that this is the week when the Lord died. One even has to work on Good Friday. In the States, religion is not a serious affair."

On the island, church-going is a social affair as well as a religious ritual. Even in the towns the church is easily available and is often the center of interest. In New York, however, many of the respondents have to work on Sundays, especially if they are in the service trades. But whether or not they work on Sundays, when we asked, "How often do you attend church?" about half of the migrants said that they never or almost never go.

TABLE VI-3. FREQUENCY OF CHURCH ATTENDANCE IN NEW YORK

Frequency of Church Attendance	Men	Women	Total
Once a week or more	29%	40%	36%
Once or twice a month	15	15	15
Almost never or never	56	45	49
TOTAL (100%)	(417)	(696)	(1113)

Women are apt to attend church more frequently than men, but there are no consistent differences among color groups or by time of arrival.

All migrants are less likely to attend church in New York than in Puerto Rico. When asked to make the comparison more than half said that they attended more often on the island, 36 per cent that there was no difference, 10 per cent that they attend more in New York. There were no consistent differences among the color groups nor according to time of arrival.

That time of arrival makes no difference would seem to indicate that the loss of religious habits does not take place as the migrant becomes more accustomed to living in New York. A migrant who joined a church upon his arrival has continued to belong. Those who have changed their religious patterns did so upon their arrival; since they would have to seek out a church, they probably had their first opportunity to evaluate church attendance for themselves.

The principal reasons given for the failure to attend church were: in Puerto Rico one "had more time to go," (62 per cent); easier access to a church in Puerto Rico (16 per cent); family pressure or because church attendance was a special requirement in Puerto Rico (13 per cent). Others referred to language difficulties or the fact that their religious convictions had changed since they left Puerto Rico.

TABLE VI-4. "WHAT IS YOUR RELIGION AND HOW DO YOU FEEL ABOUT IT?"

Attitude toward Religion	Catholic	Protestant	Spiritualists & sect members	No religion
Most important	12%	24%	49%	—
Very important	32	32	33	—
I'm religious in my own fashion	56	44	18	95
Against religion	—	—	—	5
TOTAL (100%)[a]	(922)	(103)	(67)	(19)

[a] Excludes 2 respondents who did not report on their attitude to religion.

One's intimate attitude toward religion is more important psychologically than declarations of formal religious affiliation or frequency of church attendance. When asked, "Which best describes the way you feel about religion?" about 53 per cent, said, "I am religious in my own fashion"; 32 per cent that religion was very important, and 15 per cent that it is the most important thing in their lives.

The Catholics are more likely than any other group to say that they are "religious in their own fashion," 56 per cent compared with 44 per cent of the Protestants, and 18 per cent of the Spiritualist and sect members. Not many Catholics, therefore, say that religion is "the most important thing" in their lives: only 12 per cent take this position, compared with 24 per cent of the Protestants and 49 per cent of the Spiritualists and sect members.

TABLE VI-5. PROPORTIONS WHO THINK RELIGION IS VERY OR MOST IMPORTANT IN THEIR LIVES, BY SEX AND CHURCH ATTENDANCE

	Once a week or more	Once or twice a month	Almost never or never
Women	76%	46%	30%
Men	83%	38%	20%
TOTAL	78%	43%	26%

The subjective feeling that religion is important and the objective reports on church attendence are closely related. Seventy-eight per cent of all those who attend church once a week or more, but only 26 per cent of those who seldom or never attend church, feel that religion has a high importance in their lives.

TABLE VI-6. PROPORTIONS WHO THINK RELIGION VERY OR MOST IMPORTANT IN THEIR LIVES, BY TIME OF ARRIVAL AND SEX

	Recent	Early
Women	58%	46%
Men	43%	39%
TOTAL	52%	44%

More women than men believe religion is important to them; with the exception of those who attend church most frequently. If the men attend church once a week or more, they take their religion more seriously than the women. Racial differences toward religion appear strongly only among the women, where 26 per cent of the intermediates against 16 or 17 per cent of the white and Negro women, feel that religion is very important to them. Among both men and women, and all racial groups, those who have been in New York longer tend to place less importance on religion.

It is often said that migrants generally turn to their religious organizations in the hope that they will provide orientation in a new and bewildering world. This is a two-way process: the migrant clings to his language and his religion because he seeks secure and familiar things in an unfamiliar environment; but the more he clings, the less chance he has of enlarging his new world. As the Puerto Rican migrant feels more at home in New York, his intimate attitude to religion gradually slackens off.

7

Even in time of need, the migrant is generally reluctant to approach an institution for help. He is accustomed to depending on his friends or relatives, whether the problem is unemployment, lack of funds, or family troubles. Even Puerto Ricans who have been in New York a relatively long time continue to rely most strongly on family and other informal assistance, although some do learn to seek agency help. In the medical field, there is less reluctance to seek help and more familiarity with New York's institutions, but on the whole, the migrants either do not know about, or do not care to use, city agencies and institutions.

On the island, welfare services, until recently almost completely absent, are still handicapped by lack of funds and leave wide gaps in the services needed; reliance was placed on personal help, which has the status of a religious act. Thus, the Puerto Rican in New York City who comes in contact with an agency finds an unfamiliar pattern. If he receives money and service, he often feels that he is encountering a new kind of generosity. But along with this largess there are certain inconveniences: to the Puerto Rican, case workers may seem to have an obsession about prying into personal affairs and getting people to change their habits, customs, and beliefs. The case worker may sometimes seem the only obstacle between the Puerto Rican's learned expectations and the helpful wealth of the agency. She is seen as an inconvenience to be coped with by a matching of wits. If, on the other hand, the case worker seems easily satisfied with the client's superficial statement of need, she may look like a sister of mercy, and there is a temptation to drop in her lap all problems and troubles.

Most of the 43 per cent of the migrants who said they had troubles were concerned with problems of health. Next in importance were economic and financial troubles. The recent migrants, particularly the intermediate racial group, are most likely to admit having troubles. One half of the newcomers—both men and women—but only one third of the older residents admit that they have worries in New York.

TABLE VI-7. SPONTANEOUSLY MENTIONED TROUBLES AND ACTIVITIES ENGAGED IN

Remedy	Financial	Housing	Family	Health
Personal effort	91%	78%	61%	18%
Institution	3	16	15	39
Friends or family	3	3	3	42
All other	3	3	3	1
TOTAL[b] (100%)	(66)	(36)	21[a]	(143)

[a] These 21 per cent "other" are mainly those who say they are going back to Puerto Rico.

[b] Excludes 585 cases who had no troubles; 98 cases who did not answer the question on troubles; and 131 who were not doing anything about their troubles, or did not say what they were doing.

Those who admitted to having troubles were asked, "What are you doing about them?" For the most part, they think in terms of solving their problems privately; only 23 per cent of the migrants who have troubles think in terms of institutional aid. If we cross-classify the troubles named with the activities pursued in search of relief from them, we find that institutions are looked to mainly for help in medical problems. On financial problems, 91 per cent say they intend to rely on their own efforts.

The longer the Puerto Ricans have been residents in New York, the more likely they are—especially the women—to think in terms of agency assistance for their problems. Only 19 per cent of the recently arrived women, but 33 per cent of the earlier arrived women say that they would turn to agencies. Indeed, the older residents among the women are almost as likely to turn to agencies (33 per cent) as to rely on personal effort (39 per cent). Although the number of cases is really too small to furnish reliable differences, it appears that the women in the intermediate racial group are the most likely to learn to rely upon agency help. Almost half the women in this racial group, who are old residents of the city, say that they would depend upon agency assistance for help in time of trouble.

These figures suggest that the Puerto Rican does not expect to depend upon a larger, formal world for aid for his troubles. Yet, with all this, various welfare institutions are part of a secondary world of which the migrants are aware. When asked if they *know* of any agencies which might help them, 94 per cent are aware of health facilities, 73 per cent of employment agencies, 50 per cent know about institutions offering financial aid, and 36 per cent of day care for children. Of course the actual existence or availability of facilities influences these answers.*

* Police activity is generally greater in the slums than in other urban areas. We asked our sample, "Since you have been living in New York, have you called the police for help or for any other reason?" Eighty-seven per cent had never called the police. Many reasons given by the 13 per cent, who had shown a high degree of reliance upon the police as an available personnel of authority, were for other than law enforcement, although that did rank highest (41 per cent). Other reasons were: to call an ambulance (33 per cent); to ask information about a hospital or other such service (15 per cent); to resolve trouble within family, e.g., husband-wife quarrel (7 per cent); or report a missing person (4 per cent).

To a related question—"Since you have been living in New York, have you ever been in court for anything?"—11 per cent said, "Yes," 89 per cent, "No." Some 36 per cent of those who had been in a New York court had been involved in family court proceedings; 30 per cent had been plaintiffs in civil suits; the remaining cases were scattered. All these migrants were asked, "Did you get help from anyone?" Only 34 per cent had obtained a private lawyer, only 9 per cent help from a legal aid society, 14 per cent help from social agencies. Twenty-one per cent were helped only by friends and relatives

Most people who know a place where they can get help learned of it through friends or relatives. This varies from a high of 75 per cent in the case of financial aid to a low of 49 per cent in day-care facilities for children. The latter field shows the highest proportion of referrals by other agencies, partly because help has been sought at schools.

8

The outermost reaches of the Puerto Rican world are filled with the sights and sounds of the media of mass communication; the magazines and newspapers, radio and movies. Like the rest of their world, these formal media are partly Spanish and partly American. And as among other low-income groups, the media to which they are exposed frequently distort, rather than clarify what is happening in this world, or orient anyone to his place in it.

It may be that since the Puerto Rican does not possess the full context of American life, as do those who grow up on the continent, he accepts the content and implicit values of the mass media less critically than the continental, and is more open to the suggestions of feelings and conduct which it offers. In striving to be at home in a new environment, he may all the more easily develop a false base of security. At any rate, these formal media enable the stranger to acquire a common apperceptive mass with continentals similarly exposed, and thus share with other Americans the same standardized inner life.

The Puerto Ricans in New York use the radio and newspaper more than they do movies or magazines. The reason for these habits are directly related to the low educational and income level of the Puerto Ricans.

In Puerto Rico, the radio at the crossroads *colmado* or *cantina* is often the focus of the neighborhood, and migrants carry their radio habit with them. In New York City as a whole including all income ranges, 98 per cent of all migrant families have radios. This lends credence to the popular story that the first thing a

Puerto Rican does upon arriving in New York is to buy a radio.

Once the migrant has made the initial investment, radio listening is cheap. Seventy-seven per cent of the Puerto Ricans in the core areas listen to the radio after six P.M., only 8 per cent listen to early morning programs, and 6 per cent tune in during the day. In general, this pattern follows the listening pattern of the U.S. population as a whole, but it also reflects the high degree of employment away from home during the day.

Over two-thirds of the migrants (71 per cent) prefer Spanish radio programs; 18 per cent choose to listen to American programs; 11 per cent express no preference. While there are several Spanish-language programs after 6:00 P.M. and a new evening program at 9:00 P.M. there are few such programs during the day. Only 7 per cent of the Puerto Rican housewives listen to the radio during the day, in marked contrast to the listening habits of the American housewife in general. The Puerto Rican housewife is less apt to know English and hence, in her lack of daytime listening, finds another constriction.

Newspapers are read at least once a week by 84 per cent of the sample. Thirty-four per cent of all the migrants read New York English daily papers, 22 per cent Spanish language papers, and 28 per cent, both.

Following the pattern of most low-income and education groups in their newspaper habits, the Puerto Ricans read the cheaper and more sensational papers: 67 per cent read the tabloid *Daily News*. The other English language papers had only scattered readers: 13 per cent read the *Journal-American*, and 10 per cent the *Mirror*. Of the several Spanish language papers available in New York, *La Prensa* was read by 48 per cent of the 930 readers of newspapers; although not owned by Puerto Ricans, it devotes considerable space to activities on the island and to the social life of Puerto Ricans in New York. *El Mundo* and *Imparcial*, both published in Puerto Rico, are read by 5 and 11 per cent respectively. There are several other smaller Spanish papers published by Puerto Ricans in New York, but altogether these are read by only 6 per cent of the respondents.

TABLE VI-8. NEWSPAPERS READ BY MIGRANTS

Newspaper[a]	Percentage who read each paper
New York Daily News	67%
La Prensa	48
New York Journal-American	13
El Imparcial (San Juan)	11
New York Mirror	10
New York Times	8
El Mundo (San Juan)	5
Other Spanish papers	6
Other English papers	7
TOTAL READING NEWSPAPERS AT LEAST ONCE A WEEK.[b]	(930)

[a] A new Spanish daily *El Diavia de Nueva York,* began publication a few months after this survey was completed.

[b] The percentages add to more than 100 since some respondents read more than one newspaper a week.

Fifty-two per cent of the respondents go to movies once a week or more, 11 per cent attend less than that, and 37 per cent almost never or not at all. To those 52 per cent, movies offer escape from the cold and from hard work. For a few hours the realities of their life in New York can be left outside the box office; they can participate in adventure, glamour, and stories with happy endings. Many of the Puerto Ricans know the names of all the current movie stars. Some of them, in fact, report that they go for treatment to the Bette Davis Hospital (the Beth-David)!

Whether they attend movies frequently or not, 46 per cent of all the migrants prefer Spanish films, 35 per cent the American, and 19 per cent express no preference. The Spanish-speaking core areas of New York have several movie houses where only Latin-American films are shown, but the preference for Spanish-language movies is not as marked as the level of comprehension of the English language might indicate. Incomplete understanding of the sound tract is no great barrier to the understanding of many American movies.

Of all the mass media, the Puerto Ricans are exposed to magazines the least. Because magazines usually cost more, and generally require an educational level higher than do tabloid newspapers, and perhaps most importantly, because few magazines in Spanish are available in New York, such a result is to be expected.

Forty-three per cent of all the migrants said that they read magazines more or less frequently, 29 per cent read English magazines, 9 per cent read Spanish, and 5 per cent read both. Over half of the migrants (57 per cent) did not usually read any magazines.

The islanders' total exposure to these media of mass communication is rather superficial. It is as if they permitted themselves to be touched in a brief and casual way by one or another of these media as the only means available to secure news or amusement—and not because the tendency to turn to the newspaper, movies, radio, or magazines is an intrinsic part of their behavior patterns. These media offer to the several types of masses in New York the lowest common denominator of participation in American culture, or at least in American mass culture. When they enter the city, the Puerto Ricans enter this world too; but even on this most external level they do not participate much in America's mass culture.

From the responses to the questions on the four mass media mentioned, an index of exposure to mass media was built.[12] Such an index can be used only relatively, for it is only a crude estimate of exposure to mass media revealed by answers to rather formal questions. But, even by means of this rating, only 25 per cent of the migrants have been "highly exposed" to mass media —reading at least one magazine more or less frequently, going to the movies about once a week, reading at least one newspaper at least once a week, and listening to the radio somewhat regularly. Very few migrants (3 per cent) are at the other extreme of never being exposed to any of these four media, but following a scale of exposure, 35 per cent of the migrants rank intermediate and 40 per cent rank lowest.

Education is a decisive factor in exposure to mass media: 47 per cent of those who have attended school to the sixth grade or beyond are highly exposed as against only 18 per cent of those who attended up to the fifth grade or less. There are no differences according to sex. As the migrant lives in the city longer, he becomes more exposed, or develops wider habits of attention to mass media; but this is true only among the more highly educated.

TABLE VI-9. PROPORTIONS HIGHLY EXPOSED TO MASS
MEDIA BY EDUCATION, SEX, AND TIME OF ARRIVAL

	Education			
	High		Low	
Time of Arrival	Men	Women	Men	Women
Early	39%	40%	10%	10%
Recent	27%	29%	10%	7%

Among the less educated, practically the same proportions, men or women, recently arrived or not, are highly exposed to mass media. Among the higher educated, however, time of arrival makes a more noticeable difference, raising the proportions of highly exposed from 27 or 29 per cent to 40 per cent.

Thus, the chances that a poorly educated migrant will become exposed to the mass media are only about one in ten. This is both good and bad for the migrant. His lack of education does keep him away from the somewhat dubious cultural level of mass media; but it also keeps him from whatever benefits there may be—personal enjoyment, general informational awareness of his new world, contact in any world wider than his immediate household, and whatever chance of assimilation mass media provide.

9

The center of the Puerto Rican world in New York City is the immediate kinship group, the extended ritual kinship relations, and the home town friends who are members of the household. Stretching out from this center are relations, first, with friends and relatives having locality connections and living in the same apartment house and, second, with friends in the same building not from the same island locality. From here, the Puerto Rican world spills out into the street, to more or less casual cliques in bars and restaurants and grocery stores. The migrant may pick up friends at the place where he works or in the few organizations to which he so seldom belongs, but in general his effective social world, the one from which he gains such security as he has, is confined to the household, the apartment house, and the street.

Beyond these, the migrants' social world usually becomes impersonal and casual and distant and confusing. He may hang around a travel agency; he is aware of police officers; there is a pretty good chance that he belongs to a labor union; he may be aware of, if not in contact with, the school his child goes to, with social welfare agencies or very rarely with a settlement house. Relations within and with the members of organizations are rare; for most migrants they do not exist. What he knows about the city, apart from his personal relations bounded by his street and his job, he knows only from the cheaper sensational mass media of communication; these bring to him the highly selected and often distorted contents of the American world he is trying to fit together and himself into.

Yet the migrant is not entirely alone in the city. In the core areas, he is inside a loose ethnic grouping of households—an unorganized ghetto which is somewhere between the world he has left and the bottom level of the society he has begun to enter. The change is still an acute one, but it could be unbearable were it not that special worlds, Spanish Harlem and the Bronx's Morrisania, arise to protect him from the greater shock of the full stream of strident United States life. Further, like all lower-class people the members of this world are not expected to participate as fully in the major conventional routine.

The Puerto Rican migrant in New York is no longer living in a community in the sense of a shared life in a familiar area. This isolation of the individual, generally characteristic of modern metropolitan society, becomes all the more acute for the migrant, a man or woman on the cultural margins of two worlds.

There is a positive side. Personal freedom has increased. Yet in many cases, freedom and psychic security are in tension. The tight social control of smaller communities is often a felt constraint, especially to those with new ideas or ambitions that go beyond the narrow limits; yet for many others control is a great comfort. This tension comes out strongly at the center of the Puerto Rican world; the family itself is in many instances disrupted. Children no longer get as much attention from the mother and may, in their freedom, feel rejected; women, as well as men, realize that they are no longer as dependent on each other as before. For many Puerto Ricans, New York may provide escape from rigid moral standards, but along with this there is the feeling of being lost in a large world where people do not know or care very much about each other. Guilt feelings are aroused in some migrants by actions which would not be countenanced at home; others may reject the new pattern completely and overemphasize their own rigidities. There may be a gradual acceptance of the new situation, a superficial adjustment which causes only occasional trouble, but this adjustment may itself be a threat to personal security.

The story of the Puerto Rican world in New York is an old story in America, a story not only of migrants from Europe, but also of America's small town and rural people entering into the life of its great cities. The tension of freedom and insecurity which accompanies every moving group is, for the present generation of Puerto Ricans, further complicated by the lateness of their entry into this society's life. The larger scene in which the Puerto Ricans enact their journey is not the expanding, hopeful society of pre-World War I days; it is the contracting world of a city built of migrations whose people may already have closed off the classic ways of becoming Americans.

7.　　　　　*Conflict and Solidarity*

THE Puerto Rican migrant, a product of cultural and racial conflict on his island, produces further ethnic conflict in New York
City; he is a victim of both conflicts, and, like most people caught
in ethnic diversity, he sometimes turns on his own group to rend
it, and in so doing, further victimizes himself.

The deep split and sharp tension between island Spanish and
continental American ways are emphasized in the marginal situation of Puerto Rico. From a somewhat philistine point of view,
one professional observer has neatly described the conflict: "Each
group is criticized and abused by the other for the display of
traits it considers to be virtues; the terms that one uses to enumerate the virtues are used by the other as epithets to describe the
vices. The American is realistic, concise, exact, irreverent, competent, prompt, and dependable; the Puerto Rican tends to be
romantic, diffuse, vague, superstitious, inefficient, dilatory, and
unreliable. Where the American is modern, the Puerto Rican
is medieval; where the American is scientific, the Puerto Rican
is poetic. . . . The American is impatient with the casual attitudes
of the Puerto Rican; the Puerto Rican is irritated by the exacting
demands of the Americano."[1]

Entering a New York slum, where ethnic conflict is always
likely to be sharp, or Harlem, where racial struggle is not hidden,
hearing the classic migratory rhetoric, as well as the anti-Negro,
the Puerto Rican migrant becomes uneasily aware of the facts
of life for minority people in America. Only very generally can
the Puerto Rican ethnic and racial problem in New York be
spoken of as a task of "harmonizing the life of the immigrants

with our own," which is the way students spoke of immigrations twenty-five years ago.[2] Certainly for these migrants, many of whom are Negroes, "ours" is not a harmonious life but precisely the opposite. To the New Yorker fresh from Texas, for example, behavior on the lower East Side is every bit as strange as that in Spanish Harlem. For many situations there is no common definition which could be learned by a would-be adaptive man; as he remains in the city, he merely learns new ethnic and social prejudices. In the Puerto Rican story, ethnic, social, and cultural conflict inevitably looms large.

In our interviews, we found that Puerto Ricans had strong feelings of being rejected by non-Puerto Ricans and that, with the usual appellations, they returned the antagonisms: "The Italians are no good. They are ignorant and low-class. They are gangsters." "The Irish are drunks." "The Latin-Americans are jealous of us." "Jewish storekeepers exploit us. The poorest they have in the store is good enough for the Puerto Rican." "The Negroes are ruffians. It is not safe to walk through the park at night." "Americans consider themselves superior. All they care about is the dollar."

As product, producer, and victim of ethnic antagonism, the Puerto Rican in New York may turn upon people from his own birthplace. The Puerto Rican world is not unified; it does not produce strong feelings of solidarity, at least none more specific than the general slogans of national pride: "The worst thing that can happen is to work for a Puerto Rican." "Puerto Ricans change here." "It is the lower class of Puerto Ricans who have now come here from the island."

I

To the over-all question, "In your opinion, do Americans generally like or dislike the Puerto Ricans here in New York?" 39 per cent of the migrants in the core settlements answered, "Like," 45 per cent answered, "Dislike," and 16 per cent said, "Don't know." The high percentage of "Don't know" answers does not necessarily indicate an absence of opinion, but rather a reluctance to answer questions on a highly emotional topic.

The men seem to feel slightly more secure than the women: 44 per cent of the men, compared with 37 per cent of the women, declare that Americans like Puerto Ricans; 10 per cent of the men but 19 per cent of the women are unwilling to commit themselves. Racial differences, however, are more important than differences between the sexes.

More of the white Puerto Ricans than the Negro, and more of the Negro than the intermediate group, assert that Americans like Puerto Ricans. The two colored groups, however, do not declare outright that Americans *dislike* Puerto Ricans; they seek refuge in noncommittal answers. Among both men and women, the intermediate and Negro migrants are more apt to avoid the question by saying they "don't know"; this may point to an insecurity on the part of the colored, which is even stronger among the intermediate women.

TABLE VII-1. "Do Americans Like Puerto Ricans?" by Sex and Color

Do Americans Like Puerto Ricans?	Males			Females		
	White	Intermediate	Colored	White	Intermediate	Colored
Like	46%	30%	50%	40%	29%	33%
Dislike	46	57	34	44	44	43
Don't know	8	13	16	16	27	24
Total (100%)	(293)	(57)	(65)	(418)	(117)	(160)

More intermediate men express opinions on the subject than intermediate women—in fact, more than any other group in the sample—57 per cent declaring categorically that Americans dislike Puerto Ricans. The intermediately colored women are equally unwilling to say that Americans like Puerto Ricans, but they are more likely than any other group to avoid making a decision: 27 per cent as compared with 16 per cent of the white women and 24 per cent of the colored women.

There are certain trends among the colonists according to how long they have been in New York City. The colored men—both intermediate and Negro—more and more come to feel that Americans don't like the Puerto Ricans, although the white Puerto Ricans show no such trend. Among the women, only the intermediate group seem, in the course of their New York residence, to come to feel that Americans don't like Puerto Ricans; the Negro and the white show no trend.

Such a "sponge" question as the one just presented is used mainly to lead to the reasons migrants will give for their opinions. Those who thought Americans dislike Puerto Ricans were asked for their reasons. In justifying their assertions, only 7 per cent mention personal experience; 41 per cent refer to experiences which have been reported to them, either by other people or by the press.

These reports impress slightly over 40 per cent of the migrants, who feel dislike from Americans. The only notable exception is the intermediate men—the grifos and the indios. If it is true that all color groups have been equally exposed to such reports, apparently these are the most sensitive to them. One out of every four colored men and one out of every three white men is impressed with these experiences, but better than six out of every ten of the intermediate men dwell upon and remember the stories that have been circulated in the Puerto Rican community about the prejudice Puerto Ricans have encountered in New York.

Intermediates are also more antagonistic to New Yorkers than either whites or Negroes. To account for Americans' dislike of them, 14 per cent of the intermediate men and 12 per cent of the intermediate women ascribe unpleasant qualities to New Yorkers: they are snobbish and disagreeable, intolerant, stupid. The corresponding proportions of white and Negro men are 8 per cent of both groups; of white and Negro women, 7 and 3 per cent, respectively.[3]

These intermediately colored are also the most articulate in giving their reasons; the Negroes the least articulate. Of those who think Americans dislike them, about half of the Negro and

white groups, but only 10 per cent of the intermediate, refuse
to say why they think so.

The general question of whether Americans like or dislike
Puerto Ricans is tied up with the question of whether they think
Puerto Ricans are "inferior." Among the migrants, opinion on
this question runs like this: 31 per cent feel that "all or many"
Americans "consider Puerto Ricans to be inferior"; 47 per cent
feel that this statement applies to some Americans; 12 per cent
to none; while 10 per cent did not answer the question.

Men tend to be more sensitive to the imputed antagonism
than women. About one out of every three men says that many
Americans deprecate Puerto Ricans, but only about one out of
four women do so. This does not mean that more women feel
accepted but that they prefer to say they "don't know." Twice
as many women as men refuse to commit themselves.

It is the colored group—and again, particularly the intermediate respondents—who are most likely to express this feeling. Both men and women in the marginal color group are more
likely than either whites or Negroes to say that many Americans
consider Puerto Ricans inferior.[4]

After being here a while, men of all color groups come to feel
that they are rejected as inferior by Americans. White women
do not, but colored women, especially the intermediately colored,
do.

Those who think Americans dislike Puerto Ricans are also
apt to think that *many* Americans consider Puerto Ricans inferior: 58 per cent of these, but only 8 per cent of those who
think Americans like them.

2

The Puerto Rican migrants, living in the slums of the Bronx
and Manhattan, find themselves side by side with other minority
ethnic groups. Aside from the physical isolation of such groups
in these ghettos, as New Yorkers, at work and on the streets, they

come into contact with the many minorities that make up the ethnic and racial strata of New York City.

For the migrant who is accustomed to the national background of the island—that is, to its centuries-old Spanish heritage—to be plunged into the motley New York scene is a new experience. Although this background is culturally heterogeneous, it is a heterogeneity with which Puerto Ricans are familiar. Some of the migrants had never met a Jew until they came to New York; many had never met an Italian until they arrived in New York and found themselves neighbors. Once in New York they became aware of the other ethnic minorities. Finding themselves a focus of antiminority feeling, they may, in turn, begin to take on prejudices against other groups.

But, for the most part, they are bewildered by the presence of so many ethnic and culture groups; only slowly do they acquire a mild sort of antagonism. Even the anti-Negro feeling which the Puerto Rican knows on the island is much different in quality, is a much more subtle discrimination, than the continental prejudice. In most activities he is treated more as an individual and less as the representative of a racial group; areas closed to the Negro on the island are mainly spheres of élite social circulation. Race-conscious Puerto Ricans find it easy on the island to pretend to themselves that for them even the subtle type of discrimination does not exist. Anti-Negro feeling is the prejudice they absorb most readily in New York, but even this is not widespread in the migrant community.

That the migrants do not absorb ethnic group prejudice to any great extent is indicated by their willingness to work with other ethnic groups. Very few migrants declare that they do not like to work with a series of specified ethnic groups. The Negro minority is the only one singled out for relative disapproval; but even here the proportion who say that they dislike working with Negroes is low (20 per cent). And on this, as on all ethnic questions, the typical migrant says that he has no preferences either way.

There are even less feelings of antagonism towards Italians; only 10 per cent say that they dislike working with Italians. They are also more likely to express a positive feeling towards Italians: 26 per cent say they like the idea of working with Italians compared with the 18 per cent who express a positive feeling towards working with Negroes.

Only a handful declare that they dislike working with Americans and other Puerto Ricans, and it is here that the greatest proportion report an outright liking. But even so, many are still likely to say "it doesn't matter."

Whatever feelings of prejudice the migrant Puerto Ricans express exist among the whites and Negroes with very little variation. There is a certain softening of anti-Negro feeling among the colored compared with the white Puerto Ricans in the sense that they are more willing to express a preference for working with Negroes. Generally, the mild sort of prejudice which the Puerto Ricans learn in New York flourishes more among the women than among the men, despite the fact that more women than men refrain from answering the questions on the various ethnic and racial groups. The white women are most antagonistic to the Negroes; among the men, however, equal proportions of both white and colored men say that they dislike working with Negroes.

The same feelings exist to a lesser extent with respect to Italians. Here, too, the colored Puerto Ricans are more likely than the whites to express a positive attitude toward Italians. But the women, regardless of race, are less likely to "like" Italians than are the men. The general pattern, however, is to be non-committal.

The most clear-cut preference for any group was expressed by the intermediate migrants, particularly the intermediate men. Only when the intermediate migrants are questioned about working with other Puerto Ricans is the noncommittal answer not the most prevalent. Compared with less than 40 per cent of all the other migrants, 53 per cent of the intermediate men, and 45 per cent of the intermediate women, say that they like very much to work with other Puerto Ricans. Because of his ambiguous racial position, the intermediate Puerto Rican may feel that only among other Puerto Ricans can he cash in on the margin of social superiority to which he feels his light skin or Caucasian features entitle him.[5]

Certain preferences for working with other ethnic and racial groups change in the course of the migrants' residence in New York. Negro men and women learn in time to dislike working with other Puerto Ricans, and the Negro women become less likely to object to working with other Negroes, perhaps because they may be more privileged among American Negroes than among other Puerto Ricans. The intermediate and white women follow the Negro women in learning to dislike working with other Puerto Ricans, and the intermediate women, like the Negro women, grow to prefer working with the Negroes. The intermediate and white men, on the other hand, learn to dislike working with the Negroes—the intermediate, perhaps in a reaction to being stereotyped with them; the white, perhaps picking up the prevailing prejudices of other types of New Yorkers against Negroes.[6]

3

In discussing the Puerto Rican world, we indicated that it was a fragmented, disunited sphere for social living; that it was without a wide net of organizations, without effective Puerto Rican leadership, and that there were evidences of internal class splits within it. We also indicated that New York's general culture was racially split, and thus it was difficult—to the extent that "assimilation" was made difficult—for a unified community to arise.

It is a confused situation. In some areas of Harlem, Negroes and Puerto Ricans, neither wishing to be identified with the other, are in frequent and bitter conflict. Should the economy slip, should peace with slump break out, many competent observers believe there would be serious trouble. On the other hand, it is reliably reported that some American Negroes in Harlem are attempting to learn Spanish!

When he comes to New York, the Puerto Rican migrant is either plunged into one of two worlds, or must exist between them. If he is white, he must adjust himself to the white culture of New York; if he is not white, he has no choice but to blend into the Negro community. The white migrant must take on the behavior and values of white America. The colored migrant finds that the world to which he must adapt himself is the Negroes' America.

For those in the intermediate racial classification—the indio or grifo—the position is more difficult. The Negro with "good" features or with Negro features but light skin, hair, and eyes, in Puerto Rico was likely to have held a position somewhat above the darker Negro—a world somewhere between the colored and the white worlds. He made a distinction between himself and the dark Negro, which was recognized by others to an extent which depended mainly upon his specific personal aspirations and achievements. In New York he finds this margin of privilege no longer acknowledged. To the continental, white or colored, he is a Negro. If he is to "assimilate," it means that he must "become like" the Negro in the metropolitan community. The world in which he is to function inconspicuously is the Negro world. It makes no difference whether he is light- or dark-skinned or has "good" or "bad" features and hair. He finds that he can hold only certain jobs, mix socially only with certain people. Almost always he must live in the Harlem ghetto, or in certain Negro sections of the Bronx.

Although no other community will accept him, the intermediately colored migrant is frequently unwilling to identify himself with the Negro community. If there were sufficient numbers of people like him and if his feelings of uneasiness were explicit, he might be able to form his own "community," but to so small a minority such recourse is lacking. Whether or not he is conscious of it, the intermediate migrant has less motivation, or incentive, to "adjust himself" to New York life. He has little motivation to make friends; the customs of America seem even stranger and more bewildering to him than to either the white or the clearly Negro migrant. He has a stronger feeling of not being accepted by the New York world. He is more sensitive to slights, more alert to discriminating experiences, although he feels them to have been directed against all Puerto Ricans. More than the others, he feels that Americans look down upon Puerto Ricans. In the same way, he becomes more quickly aware of the identity of other ethnic minorities within the city and he is more likely to take on prejudices against them. He finds that if he learns English, he is even more likely to lose the slight advantage he holds in New York over the American Negro—for somehow a non-American Negro receives privileged treatment in the New York community. For this reason he is less likely to know English well and he is more likely to use Spanish in public places so that he will be identified not as a Negro but as a Latin. Confronted by painful contradictions, he suffers all the difficulties of any newcomer, and, in addition, those of a racial problem for which he is relatively untrained.

This is by no means to say that similar problems of adjustment do not exist among white and colored Puerto Ricans, but that there are strong indications that among the intermediate group these problems of adjustment are more acute. Thus, it is probable that their problems of adjustment are likely to persist for a longer period of time.

We asked one final set of ethnic questions that throw additional light on the position of the intermediately colored Puerto Ricans, their self-images, and the general problem of Puerto Rican unity. It is not enough to know the feeling Americans are believed to have; since the Puerto Ricans live among other ethnic and racial minority groups, we must get closer to their frame of comparison. As we wanted to know whether they felt that they received better or worse treatment than other minority groups, we therefore asked, "Do Americans treat Puerto Ricans better or worse than Negroes? . . . Jews? . . . Italians? . . . Other Latins?"

The Puerto Ricans as a whole do not readily express a feeling that they receive better or worse treatment than other ethnic groups: regardless of which ethnic minority they are asked to compare their treatment with, their answer is, characteristically, "Equal"—"The Same." Additionally, a high proportion of migrants say they don't know how to answer the question. Even though it is the women, more than the men, who again tend to avoid expressing their ideas, this can hardly be interpreted as a lack of awareness of New York's definition of these ethnic minorities, since the same high proportion indicate that they "don't know" if they receive better or worse treatment than other Latins with whom they strongly identify. Third, note that the one group over which most migrants feel they are preferred is the Negro minority. But even here their answers are predominantly "equal."

TABLE VII-2. TREATMENT OF PUERTO RICANS COMPARED WITH THAT OF OTHER ETHNIC AND RACIAL GROUPS

Compared with other ethnic groups Puerto Ricans are treated	Negroes	Jews	Italians	Other Latins
Better	22%	11%	11%	7%
Same	47	41	45	66
Worse	16	29	24	10
Don't know	15	19	20	17
TOTAL (100%)	(1096)	(1098)	(1090)	(1087)

Colored and white migrants are in general agreement on this point, but members of the intermediate racial group break the pattern on two significant counts: (1) They are the least willing to express an opinion; among men and among women, on every ethnic group, the intermediately colored show a higher "don't know" than either Negro or white; (2) they deviate from the general pattern with their bitterness on the Negro question. Fewer of the intermediates, both men and women, than of the

Negro or white, feel that their comparative position is better than that of the continental Negro.

Although the preponderance of answers among all migrants cluster about the noncommittal "equal," they seem to identify themselves most strongly with other Latins. Two thirds or more of every group express this opinion, compared with roughly 40 per cent who feel equal treatment with any other ethnic group. This points up statistically a finding we encountered in our intensive interviews: the possible growth of a Spanish consciousness among Puerto Ricans in New York.[7]

4

Somewhat in tension with the localism and forced individuation of the Puerto Rican world, there is coming about a growth of solidarity feelings with other Spanish-speaking peoples in New York City. This, if it should take wider hold and spread, would involve the adoption of lifeways and social values somewhat different from those prevalent in Puerto Rico but different also from those of the generalized (middle class) American.

From folkways to formal organizations, there are bits of evidence pointing towards the emergence of the Spanish consciousness and the Latino type. Folkways are slowly changing in some areas to include meals and habits more common in other Spanish-speaking areas of the western hemisphere than in Puerto Rico. These are called by the migrants "Latino" and not "Puerto Rican." Puerto Ricans join the others in celebrating Columbus Day as "el dia de la raza." Such lodges as the Amparo Latino (Odd Fellows) are also now developing, although on a small scale; in its less formal aspects the Latin solidarity is suggested by conversations among recently arrived Puerto Ricans who may call themselves "Latinos," and East Harlem, "el Barrio Latino." From an observer's report of a party, in the household of an older Puerto Rican settler in the Bronx, the following is quoted: "The musicians continued playing. The wife asked for Spanish music for the Spanish man who came. They played and danced it. Then all cheered 'Viva Espana!' Comments on 'I like to go to Spain,'

were made by two of the girls. A Mexican song was played for the
guy of New Mexico who refused to dance. The wife and another
woman threw a sombrero and did the dance. Cheers to Mexico
follows: 'and to the Latin American republics.' I approached
the Spaniard. 'Do you have many Puerto Rican friends?' He
answered: 'I am a member of the Club de Hijos de Aguadilla.'
I: 'How come?' He: 'Well, I have some friends from Aguadilla
who insisted I should join because we were like brothers, so I
did. I feel like with my own paisanos. Well, you are paisanos.
That is undeniable. Puerto Ricans will never be Americans.
Spain is still alive in all the hearts of those who were lucky
enough to have its traditions.' "

There is some conflict between other Spanish-speaking peoples
and Puerto Ricans, but it is mostly of a rather impersonal sort.
Generally it is linked with the "discredit" which Puerto Ricans
sometimes feel other Spanish-speaking people throw upon them,
especially when in trouble, by claiming to be Puerto Ricans, in
order to enjoy the rights of United States citizenship. Apparently this has come up in the past particularly with Cubans,
who attempt to enter and remain working in the country by
passing as Puerto Ricans. Some Puerto Ricans tend to blame
other Spanish groups for the reputation they feel is imputed
wrongly to the Puerto Ricans. Yet these evidences of antagonism,
or at least tension, are on the whole minor and not widespread.
They are far overshadowed by the Puerto Ricans' insistence that
when dealing with Latins they do not consider them another
ethnic group but as "belonging to our race."

This feeling of identity rests first of all on the common
language, which implies a connection that one does not have to
build, but which already exists. Friends are obviously easier to
make among those who speak one's own language. But in addition, there is a kind of abstract community feeling maintained
by the Spanish tradition in the new world, which cuts across
nationality, and which sometimes makes both groups reject
"things American." Among some of the more articulate there is
the further tie of a common enemy: they may unite in an anti-

United States policy because of the United States' past behavior in her role of "the colossus of the north."

For some Puerto Ricans, the Latino type of solidarity serves as a core of resistance to assimilation and to the hard travail attending it; it leads the Puerto Ricans towards both a non-Puerto Rican and a non-American type of adjustment, a type easier and more congenial to their previous orientation. The need for change in lifeways is thus placed within a larger pattern of conduct and feeling which serves better than the Puerto Rican pattern to ease the shock, to avoid the conflict in American society. It should be noted that this Latino pattern is a somewhat "Americanized" variety of the general pattern of Spanish culture. At least there are parallels within it that are closer to the American than are Puerto Rican cultural habits—for example, the Odd Fellows organization.

What the growth of Spanish consciousness and the identification with it most accomplish for Puerto Ricans is a rise in their status. Their self-image is better served as Latinos than as Puerto-riqueños. In their struggle to escape a minority position they can thus reach out and borrow prestige from some larger and more favored minority. If there are romantic elements in this image of themselves, if there is something of the posture in it, who can say but that such elements are a proud thing, and necessary in order to bear their kind of life?

8.   *Adaptation*

THE problem of adaptation of migrants does not arise, for the society they enter, unless (1) this society contains general norms, or norms that are consistent or homogeneous enough to constitute a standard to which individual migrants might adjust; and unless (2) it is conventionally felt that strangers *should* adapt themselves to these norms. The problem of adaptation does not arise for the individual migrant unless (3) models of adjustment are available to him and (4) he wishes to avail himself of them, to become like the others in the society which he enters.

In previous decades the norms to which the migrant was expected to adjust were those of lower middle-class life in the smaller cities, applied by the Americanization authorities or professional or conventional Americanizers. These persons did expect the migrant to adapt or become assimilated, and often provided the models of adaptation in vivid or even compelling fashion, instilling in the migrant the desire to remodel himself. Although these crusades no longer exist as part of American apparatus of social control, their personnel may be still in contact with Puerto Ricans.

At present, New York City is not a homogeneous social world, nor, from the Puerto Rican standpoint, does it offer a set of consistent and available norms to which to adapt. The confined and confining Puerto Rican world of household, apartment house, and street possesses neither unity nor scope in itself, and the other worlds alongside it are also fragmented and closed up.

There is no over-all, concrete answer to the question of what
the Puerto Rican migrant should adjust himself to.

To hold out axioms generalized from the lower middle-class
milieu, usually of smaller cities, to people of such low income as
the Puerto Ricans in New York City, would be as likely to
frustrate as to motivate them, much less add to their psychical
comfort. We note in the Puerto Rican community an absence
of clear-cut models for imitation, provided by "successful" members of some ethnically solid world of their own, other ethnic
groups, or even among the least conspicuous Yankees. In individuals we note an absence of any strong, conscious desire to
become like any one acceptable and available type. This is not
due to any rebellion (the opposite of adaptation), but simply
to the unavailability of a model, the absence of a motive.

What, then, considering these factors as well as their decreas-
ing chance to realize the classic pattern of "assimilation," can
we mean by speaking of the "adaptation" of Puerto Ricans in
New York City?

Whether or not they wish to adapt, and whether or not there
is a homogeneous society or known set of norms available to
them, relevant authorities, professionals, and conventional persons of New York City do expect conspicuous strangers, Puerto
Ricans as well as any others, to adjust. Objectively, and from
the standpoint of the society, adjustment can have only a formal
meaning: to adjust is to function inconspicuously. "Functioning" means here staying alive; "inconspicuous" means not coming to the attention of the authorities, or professionals, or conventional members of society.

While the migrant might be functioning inconspicuously, he
may be quite unhappy or even disgruntled. In so far as such
feelings might be the first phase of, or the prelude to, activity,
they become relevant to the objective meaning of adaptation:
the migrant with such attitudes might cease to function, he
might become conspicuous. From a psychological angle, tempered
perhaps by a curious kind of humanitarian morality, it is usually
felt that psychic contentment of one sort or another is necessary

for a satisfactory state of adjustment. Certainly from the stand-point of the individual involved, it must be acknowledged that the meaning of adjustment should include some kind of psychic contentment. We use this definition in order to leave for further and explicit discussion the level of aspiration that may be in-volved in the subjective meaning of adjustment.

If we put together the objective and the subjective meanings of adaptation—the situation of the migrant as judged by authori-ties, professionals, and conventional hosts, and the psychological condition of the migrant—we have an adequate minimum defini-tion of adaptation: it is inconspicuous functioning with psychic contentment.

The opposite of this state is conspicuous lack of functioning accompanied by psychic discontent. In between are two types of *mal*adaptation. In the first, the individual may be functioning inconspicuously but nevertheless be discontented: this inter-nalized maladjustment may take many forms, from inhibited rebelliousness to a high level of frustrated yet controlled aspi-ration. In the second type, the individual may be functioning badly and conspicuously yet nevertheless be contented or com-fortable psychically. This externalized maladjustment also takes several forms, ranging from the individual who happily annoys others by boisterous conformism to strident features of the society routines, to the happy-go-lucky bum.

2

The adjusted man in a society of homogeneous norms is in-conspicuous by virtue of being like all other people and hence not socially visible among them. In a society with no such homogeneous norms, but with many different social types, the individual can be inconspicuous only in terms of formal com-mon denominators. The most important of these, the language he speaks, is crucial, but not in itself sufficient. In this hetero-geneous world, the only constant representatives of society at large are the official authorities. The usual and most obvious way a person becomes conspicuous to the society as a whole is by coming to the attention of these authorities, which occurs when he causes them trouble. Thus, the Puerto Rican who doesn't understand or speak English is conspicuous as a member of a different language group, but to no greater extent than members of any other of the numerous language groups. But if he causes the authorities trouble, he then becomes conspicuous as a member of a group outside the whole of the New York world, and his conspicuousness is differentiated from all other language groups.

Both difficulty with English and trouble with the authorities and agencies probably cause psychic discontent. Even if the migrant remains well inside his Spanish world, lack of proficiency in the accepted language of the country in which he lives is a threat to his ego. When he does venture out, his lack of facility may create feelings of suspicion, anger, dejection, or hostility towards that in which he cannot participate; it may even cause him to withdraw again from the wider New York scene. Certainly, if he needs help with family problems or money troubles, to the extent that he comes to the attention of official agencies or even thinks of going to them, that entails an insecurity, which is to say, a certain amount of psychic discontent. Yet we cannot simply assume that the migrant is discomforted if he has a low proficiency on language and is apt to go to officials for help: we must be certain that in our index of adaptation we stay as close as we can to the respondent's view of his own situation. Therefore, the migrant must be asked directly whether or not he feels he has troubles.

Three fifths of the migrants have arrived in New York without the tool of language elementary for making their way inconspicuously. Yet it is necessary for many to move beyond the Puerto Rican world to go to work; in order to travel on subways or buses they must know enough English to read directions and pay the fare. Even if they have no desire to talk to strangers, they are drawn into doing so. To function inconspicuously with any degree of comfort, therefore, the Puerto Rican must know

English and must use it in public places. In private situations his use of Spanish does not affect his ease in the larger New York scene except in so far as private practice of English might effect proficiency.

In order to obtain the best measure of the migrant's knowledge of English, each respondent was asked to rate himself, "Well," "Average," "Little," or "Not at all," on each of these three questions: "How well do you understand English?" "How well do you read English?" and "How well do you think you speak English?" From the answers to these questions, an index to their knowledge of English was developed.[1] We also formed an index as to their public use of English[2] according to how frequently they said they spoke English in three contexts: "at work," "when shopping," and in "places where there are Americans." The fact that not all the migrants go to work could bias this index, were it not that the question on shopping performs an equal function for housewives.

TABLE VIII-1. PUBLIC USE OF ENGLISH, BY KNOWLEDGE OF ENGLISH

	Knowledge of English				
Public use of English	Very good	Good	Intermediate	Poor	Very poor
Very frequent	54%	30%	17%	10%	1%
Frequent	23	22	18	14	2
Intermediate	14	29	33	27	5
Rarely	7	12	17	24	9
Never	2	7	15	25	83
TOTAL (100%)	(427)	(176)	(156)	(103)	(249)

A person who has a good knowledge of English but who doesn't use it in public places may be conspicuous because he doesn't speak English where it is expected; a person who speaks English frequently in public places, but who has a poor knowledge of the language is also conspicuous by virtue of his disability. Thus, if language proficiency is to be used as an index of inconspicuousness, the two dimensions must be combined.

The strong correlation that exists between the two aspects of language proficiency is expected; but the reluctance of those who know English well to use it frequently in public is considerable. Only about half of those with very good or good knowledge of English use it at a rate equal to their knowledge. (Fifty-four per cent of those with very good knowledge use it very frequently, and 52 per cent of those with good knowledge use it very frequently or frequently.) This table may be reduced to form a scale of language proficiency.[3]

In both the wider American and the Puerto Rican worlds the individual is only conscious of official agencies and authorities when he is in trouble or thinks he will be. Likewise, the individual is conspicuous to the authorities only when he "causes trouble," and is detected by them or brought to their attention. Economic trouble is major in a money society both for the individual and for the officials. In fact, "trouble" for the official agencies is likely to be anything that costs them money, directly or as time and effort. The degree to which money trouble can make a group conspicuous has already been illustrated by the publicity given to Puerto Ricans on relief. When the individuals or groups become conspicuous to authorities, that fact is often quickly transmitted to the wider public.

In connection with employment status, we found out the numbers of migrants now on relief. Answers to other questions reveal tendencies, given certain conditions, to become conspicuous to the authorities. A person who says he would go to an agency in case of economic emergency, instead of saying he would rely on personal means, is more apt to become conspicuous, as is also a person who says that he would go to an agency for help in solving a family problem rather than talking it over with his friends. The revelation of family problems, more personal than poverty, is considered, in the general American pattern, more conspicuous. There is also considerable reason to believe that these two statements of intention would be closely related to future action, because 67 per cent of those who are on relief, but only 32 per cent of those who are not on relief, would turn to an official agency in the future if they needed money. Likewise, more of those who are on relief than of those who are not would go to an official agency in "case of problems in the family."

We combined these three closely related questions into an index of actual and potential conspicuous functioning on the part of the migrant. Although very few of the migrants are now on relief, the relationship between the three factors is strong enough for them to be combined into an index of orientation towards official agencies.[4]

TABLE VIII-2. ORIENTATIONS TOWARDS RELIEF AND OTHER PUBLIC AGENCIES

	Not now on relief			Now on relief		
	If needed help for family problems, would seek			If needed help for family problems, would seek		
If needed money, would seek	Personal help	Don't know	Agency help	Personal help	Don't know	Agency help
Personal help	59%	34%	37%	30%	9%	10%
Don't know	20	46	13	20	42	4
Agency help	21	20	50	50	49	86
TOTAL (100%)	(137)	(371)	(384)	(10)	(55)	(58)

Like every other group that has been studied, Puerto Ricans react defensively when confronted with questions concerning their psychic contentment. In addition, being under direct attack as a conspicuous group, they sometimes bend over backwards to seem happy in their relations to Americans and their life in New York. We tried, therefore, to get at the realities of psychic content or discontent in a context of detailed questions about personal family life. The respondent was asked "if he had been having any troubles"; by prefacing the question with, "Everyone has troubles," an attempt was made to place the respondent in a more universal world so that he was no longer the Puerto Rican migrant in New York City, but any man, with troubles like everyone else.

The admission of troubles seems to us a vague indication of psychic discontent or discomfort. We therefore used it in our general index of adaptation. The acknowledgement of trouble correlates with language proficiency and orientation towards official agencies.[5]

Combining our several indices—the ten questions just discussed—we made an over-all index of adaptation defined as inconspicuous functioning with psychic comfort. The relationship between the three separate indices is as follows.

TABLE VIII-3. INDEX OF LANGUAGE PROFICIENCY BY ACKNOWLEDGMENT
OF TROUBLES AND ORIENTATION TO AGENCIES

Language Proficiency	Has no troubles			Has troubles		
	Oriented to agencies			Oriented to agencies		
	No	Int.	Yes	No	Int.	Yes
High	55%	52%	44%	45%	38%	32%
Intermediate	23	23	31	28	21	23
Low	22	25	25	27	41	45
TOTAL (100%)	(372)	(79)	(134)	(209)	(54)	(167)

The factors displayed in this table were reduced into our index of adaptation,[6] which enabled us to classify the people into three groups: I. The Most Adapted; II. The Intermediate; and III. The Least Adapted. There is a correlation between the three component indices, but it can be seen from the table that language proficiency is the most important factor in this index of adaptation, having troubles is generally next in importance, and contact with official agencies the least.

3

One of the primary factors affecting adaptation is whether or not the migrant has a job. Since being on relief, which implies not having a job, is included in our index of adaptation, such a result would be expected; but eliminating those not now on relief, 51 per cent of those who have jobs, compared with 27 per cent of those who do not, score high on our index of adaptation. Over three times as large a proportion of the unemployed as the employed are least adapted.

TABLE VIII-4. ADAPTATION BY EMPLOYMENT STATUS

| Adaptation | Employed | Not employed | |
		Not on relief	On relief
Most adapted	51%	27%	4%
Intermediate	41	48	54
Least adapted	8	25	42
TOTAL (100%)	(556)	(345)	(114)

The desire or need for the migrant to adapt increases when it is necessary for him to go out into the New York world to earn a living. A person who is not employed is in less contact with the modes of conduct in New York, and is not so pressed to adapt to them. Since men are usually more apt to be working and responsible for the economic condition of the family, it is logical that they would be better adapted than women: 52 per cent of the men, but only 30 per cent of the women are well adapted. This holds true, however, whether or not the migrants are working. Here are the proportions that are most adapted according to sex and whether or not they have jobs:

TABLE VIII-5. PROPORTIONS OF MIGRANTS WHO ARE MOST ADAPTED, BY EMPLOYMENT STATUS AND SEX

| Sex | Employed | Not Employed | | Total |
		Not on relief	On relief	
Men	59%	35%	7%	52%
Women	42%	27%	3%	30%
TOTAL	51%	27%	4%	39%

Thus, having a job is more important to the problem of adaptation than sex, but in any case, men are better adapted than women. This will seem strange only to those who are unable to escape the middle-class norms: in this society, lower class women do not seem to be able to function inconspicuously unless they work. Bourgeois society, with its demands for inconspicuous functioning on the part of the lower classes, thus turns the lower class woman into an agent of work rather than a housewife, thus rending family life—the center of the Puerto Rican world—in New York City.

TABLE VIII-6.   PROPORTIONS OF MIGRANTS WHO ARE MOST ADAPTED,
BY SKILL LEVEL AND SEX

| | Employed | | | Not Employed |
Sex	Skilled or higher	Semiskilled	Unskilled	
Men	60%	70%	49%	24%
Women	56%	43%	29%	22%
TOTAL	59%	53%	39%	22%

The manner in which their confined world affects the migrants' chances for adaptation is further shown by the fact that not only do jobs cause higher adaptation, but also the type of work done. On the higher levels of skill adaptation is higher—which, however, may well be due to the simple fact that the higher levels of skill require a better knowledge of English.

Fifty-nine per cent of all migrants on the highest skill level, but 39 per cent on the unskilled, are well adapted. Since men are occupationally more mobile than women, level of skill is not as important for men at skilled or semiskilled levels as it is for women in similar occupational positions.

Differences in degree of adaptation according to skill level are in part explained by the amount of education the migrants have had, since those with more education are usually working at jobs of higher skill.

Fifty-seven per cent of those who have had at least some high school, but only about one-fifth of those who have gone up to the fifth grade or less, are well adapted.

TABLE VIII-7.   ADAPTATION BY EDUCATION

Adaptation	Some high school or more	Sixth to eighth grade	Fifth grade or less
Most adapted	57%	47%	20%
Intermediate	40	40	51
Least adapted	3	13	29
TOTAL (100%)	(260)	(340)	(415)

Probably involved in the educational difference is the fact that the more educated are better equipped to meet and understand the conditions of their new life, that is, in terms of adapting it to their own immediate needs. Also, probably the more educated are better able to meet the accepted standards of urban behavior than are the less educated, for the less educated are more apt to come from rural areas. Hence the less educated migrants are having to adapt to two things at once: a big city, and a foreign one. This educational difference applies to both men and women, but it is more important in the lives of the women. A more educated woman who is not in the labor force is more likely to be well adapted than a less educated woman who is employed.

TABLE VIII-8.   PROPORTIONS OF MIGRANTS WHO ARE MOST ADAPTED, BY EMPLOYMENT STATUS, EDUCATION, AND SEX

	Employed		Not employed	
	Education		Education	
Sex	High	Low	High	Low
Men	70%	56%	46%	23%
Women	59%	36%	45%	16%
TOTAL	66%	47%	45%	17%

Forty-five per cent of the more educated women who are not now working (practically the same proportions as among men of the same category), are most adapted, as against only 36 per cent of the less educated women in the labor force. Although having a job and the type of education both influence adaptation among both men and women; the job factor is more important for the men, while education is more important for the women.

The reason for this is twofold. First, education is of primary and first importance in setting the style of life of any individual, for it conditions the type of job that a person is likely to attain later. Hence, the better educated will use the English language more proficiently, enter the higher skilled jobs, and will have wider opportunities for acquiring such cultural and economic assets as are required for inconspicuous functioning. But Puerto Rican women with more education have less chance of obtaining a job of commensurate skill level than the men: education notwithstanding, women are clustered in semiskilled jobs, while the men are more apt to work at the higher skill levels.

Secondly, jobs are not likely to be as important to women as to men. Women are usually more emotionally and socially tied to their homes and families than to their jobs. Their patterns of life and cultural habits, instilled early by education and home environment, are apt to linger permanently, and be reinforced by the rearing of children. But for the men, work is, and usually has to be, of primary importance: the patterns of their lives are more apt and more able to conform with the kind of work they do, than with the degree of their schooling.

TABLE VIII-9. ADAPTATION BY AGE

Adaptation	Under 25	25–34	35–44	45 and over
Most adapted	50%	43%	39%	25%
Intermediate	42	43	45	49
Least adapted	8	14	16	26
TOTAL (100%)	(175)	(315)	(277)	(248)

Educational differences are closely associated with age—as younger people have usually had more opportunities for education than older. Half of the migrants under 25 years of age, but only one-fourth of those 45 years of age or over, are most adapted.

As far as we can judge (the number of cases in each group becomes rather small) this difference in adaptation according to age holds true whether or not the migrants are working or have more or less education. Here are the proportions of highly adapted migrants according to the four items discussed so far.

TABLE VIII-10. PROPORTIONS OF MIGRANTS WHO ARE MOST ADAPTED, BY EMPLOYMENT STATUS, EDUCATION, SEX, AND AGE

	Employed		Not employed	
	Education		Education	
Sex and age	High	Low	High	Low
Men				
Under 35	74%	56%	48%	29%
35 or over	64%	56%	43%	26%
Women				
Under 35	67%	38%	46%	24%
35 or over	43%	34%	43%	12%

Even though they may have only a low education, the younger people are generally better adapted than the older. For instance, 24 per cent of the young, low educated women who are not in the labor force, but only half that many older women in the same group, are most adapted.

Age is an independent factor in adaptation, since it is easier for a younger person to come to another country and change his mode of life; the older person is more set in the ways of his former world, and no longer has the resiliency with which to meet partial or complete life changes and successfully adapt to them.

The intermediately colored are the least adapted of all the racial groups. The facts of migration present problems to them that the whites or Negroes do not have to face so crucially.

About three times as many of the men in the intermediate racial group score low on adaptation as do the white or Negro men. This seems to be the case in the various educational, age, and occupational groups, although there are too few of the intermediate category in our sample to present any reliable percentages.

TABLE VIII-11.   ADAPTATION, BY SEX AND RACE

	Men			Women		
Adaptation	White	Inter-mediate	Negro	White	Inter-mediate	Negro
Most adapted	55%	32%	54%	32%	28%	26%
Intermediate	35	40	37	48	45	58
Least adapted	10	28	9	20	27	16
TOTAL (100%)	(282)	(57)	(69)	(383)	(89)	(135)

Lacking in a model of adaptation and nonhomogeneous as the New York world is, it is harder for the intermediate groups; for them, particularly, there are no standards with which to conform. They are not accepted by the American whites and they are reluctant to enter the American Negro community. In this connection, because many of the intermediate migrants are eager to retain their use of Spanish, under our definition of adaptation they become conspicuous. Inconspicuous functioning in our terms conflicts here with the personal motives of the intermediate Puerto Rican migrant, who would rather be conspicuous as a member of a foreign language group than be conspicuous as a Negro.

4

Several major factors influence the adaptation of the Puerto Ricans of New York City: having a job, being a male, having more education, being younger in age, and being white. Other factors which might relate to adaptation are less important, or their influence is not apparent, when these five facts are considered. From knowledge of these simple facts we can estimate the chances of any given migrant to function inconspicuously with psychic contentment in his new environment.

All these factors may be condensed into an index of predisposition to adapt.[7] Those highest on the scale are white men under 35 years of age with at least some high school education and a skilled job. Those lowest are older women of intermediate color who have had little or only grammar school education and do not work.

TABLE VIII-12.   ADAPTATION BY PREDISPOSITION TO ADAPT

	Predisposition to adapt		
Adaptation	High	Intermediate	Low
Most adapted	58%	37%	21%
Intermediate	36	46	51
Least adapted	6	17	28
TOTAL (100%)	(220)	(495)	(300)

If the migrant is highly predisposed to adapt, the chances are about six out of ten that he will score high in adaptation, and less than one in ten that he will score low. If he is poorly predisposed, the chances are eight out of ten that he will be only moderately adapted or unadapted.

So far, no mention has been made of the fact that a migrant who has been in New York a longer time stands a better chance of being adapted than one who has been here only a short while.

Forty-four per cent of the earlier arrivals, but only 31 per cent of the recent, would appear to be well adapted. Such a statement assumes that all the later migrants have the same characteristics with respect to the predisposing factors as the earlier ones.

TABLE VIII-13. ADAPTATION, BY TIME OF ARRIVAL

	Time of arrival	
Adaptation	Before 1942	1942 or after
Most adapted	44%	31%
Intermediate	43	47
Least adapted	13	22
TOTAL (100%)	(580)	(435)

However, this table might show that length of residence in New York City does not affect adaptation, but rather that fewer migrants with high predisposition to adapt have come after 1942. The predisposition to adapt must therefore be controlled, as time of arrival is cross-tabulated with adaptation. When we do this, we find that regardless of the predisposing factors, the earlier arrivals are better adapted than the more recent.

TABLE VIII-14. ADAPTATION, BY PREDISPOSITION TO ADAPT AND TIME OF ARRIVAL

	Predisposition to adapt					
	High		Intermediate		Low	
Adaptation	Early arrival	Recent arrival	Early arrival	Recent arrival	Early arrival	Recent arrival
Most adapted	60%	54%	42%	32%	27%	16%
Intermediate	35	37	44	48	52	50
Least adapted	5	9	14	20	21	34
TOTAL (100%)	(142)	(78)	(272)	(223)	(166)	(134)

On all the levels of predisposition to adapt there is a slight correlation between the migrant's actual adaptation and his time of arrival. But more important than how long the Puerto Rican has been in the city, it appears, is whether or not he possesses, when he leaves the island, the gross attributes which increase his likelihood to get along in the New York milieu. A young, better educated, white male with a job is more likely to be adapted to the city than an older, intermediately colored woman who has little education and who does not work; and this holds true even if the former has been here only a short time, while the latter has been in the city for a longer period of residence.

It should be pointed out again, however, that this discussion of adaptation among the Puerto Rican migrants cannot with justification be assumed to describe the adjustment level, or even the predisposition to adjustment, of all Puerto Rican migrants in New York City. Since the sample investigated was confined to Puerto Ricans residing in New York City's two core areas, it is very likely that our investigation caught more of the unadjusted migrants, and that large numbers of the well-adjusted migrants escaped our investigators. For these better adjusted Puerto Ricans are precisely those who either settle elsewhere in the city or move from these core areas as soon as they begin to acclimate themselves to life in New York.

9. *Aspirations*

THE Puerto Rican journey to New York ends in the circumscribed worlds of Spanish Harlem and Morrisania. Neither these worlds, nor the economic transits to them, necessarily spur the migrants to make those identifications that form the classic pattern of American migration; it is as likely that they will continue to feel estranged, except for the few who gain solidarities with other thinned-out Latin American groups. In their slum dwellings the migrants, especially those of Negro racial type, become pupils and victims of ethnic conflict. For the women particularly, models of adaptation to American life are not readily available or easily come by.

For all migrant groups, the more social contacts are limited, the more crucial economic ties become. Occupations are the chief links between Puerto Ricans and New York City: white or colored, man or woman, the majority of the migrants work. Their main contact with American culture, and a primary incentive for adaptation, occurs in the economic sphere, specifically in the occupational roles each takes on. Leaving an economically restricted island, they make the journey to the city in search of occupational opportunities, but end up concentrated in, and restricted to, low-skill occupations and industries. Only a few eventually rise occupationally; the majority remain on island levels, more than a few sink lower.

Classically, other migrants to the United States, as they learned the language and customs of their new residence, began to aspire to jobs requiring a little more skill; and always they have aspired to occupational rises and educational improvements for their children. "I shall try," the expected attitude goes, "to do a little better for myself; and my children will do a lot better than I." Whether or not Puerto Ricans comply with this classic pattern is a major key to their future adaptation.

I

The Puerto Rican migrants' explicit desire to improve their own occupational position is somewhat limited. About 50 per cent aspire to some type of work other than that which they are now doing, while 23 per cent claim they are satisfied with their present position; 27 per cent could not or would not answer the question. This reluctance to recognize any specific aspirational life exists equally among those who are now in the labor force and those who are not, although in general women are a little less likely than the men to have formulated occupational aspirations.

Those who aspire to a different type of job are as likely to wish for a low as for a high skilled job. Thirty-two per cent of the migrants who prefer a different type of job specify a white-collar job; 19 per cent wish for skilled jobs; 35 per cent want semi- or unskilled jobs; 14 per cent would like any job that is different from the one they now hold. Men are much more likely than women to hope for highly skilled jobs.

TABLE IX-1. PREFERRED OCCUPATION, BY SEX

Preferred Occupation	Men	Women	Total
White collar	45%	22%	32%
Skilled	32	9	19
Semiskilled	8	45	29
Unskilled	3	9	6
Anything at all	12	15	14
TOTAL HAVING PREFERRED OCCUPATION (100%)	(231)	(321)	(552)

Forty-five per cent of the men, but only 22 per cent of the women would like to have white-collar jobs; while only 11 per cent of the men, but 54 per cent of the women, specify semi- or unskilled wageworker jobs. This difference is, in part, explained by the fact that the men are already working at higher levels of skill than the women: hence, any job they preferred would be on a higher level. More important is the fact that many women are not in the labor force; when specifying a job aspiration, they mention jobs which require little or no trained skill: they are seeking any job, as a temporary release from

TABLE IX-2. PREFERRED OCCUPATION, BY PRESENT OCCUPATION AND SEX

	Men			Women		
	In labor force		Not in labor force	In labor force		Not in labor force
Preferred occupation[a]	High	Low		High	Low	
High	93%	80%	60%	75%	45%	20%
Low	7	20	40	25	55	80
TOTAL (100%)[b]	(57)	(101)	(70)	(12)	(83)	(220)

[a] High occupations: white collar and skilled wageworker. Low occupations: semi- and unskilled wageworker, or "anything at all." The occupations are so combined because the fact that only half the migrants express a job preference makes the significance between individual occupational groups unreliable.

[b] Includes only those having a preferred occupation; and excludes 9 cases for whom present occupation is not known.

housewifely duties, or as an additional source of income. The movement of women in and out of the labor force (Chapter 4) makes any occupational aspirations they might have unstable, and since jobs are not so central in their lives as in those of men, they are more readily contented with low-status jobs.

Among both men and women, aspirations are cumulative; that is, the higher their present jobs, the higher their aspirations.

The women are more likely than the men to aspire to low-level jobs regardless of their present occupational position. On the low levels of skill, 55 per cent of the women, but only 20 per cent of the men, wish for jobs of low skill level.

For most women migrants, having aspirations means wanting a job; and they limit such aspirations to jobs in the wageworker stratum.

TABLE IX-3. PRESENT AND PREFERRED OCCUPATION, BY SEX

Present occupation	Preferred[a] occupation	Men	Women	Total
White collar	White collar	10%	2%	6%
Not in labor force	White collar	9	11	10
Wagework	White collar	29	9	18
Wagework	Wagework	30	19	23
Not in labor force	Wagework	22	59	43
TOTAL HAVING PREFERRED OCCUP.[b] (100%)		(228)	(315)	(543)

[a] "Anything at all" classified as wagework.
[b] Excludes 9 cases for whom present occupation is not known.

The men have more diversified aspirations; many are now wageworkers and aspire to white-collar jobs; but quite a few have no jobs now, and like the women, aspire to a wagework job. Thirty per cent of the men and 19 per cent of the women now work and have aspirations on the wageworker level, but more men than women aspire *upward* within it, 17 per cent of the men compared with only 4 per cent of the women.*

2

When the migrants who had aspirations were asked to estimate their chances of obtaining them, 30 per cent thought

* In this section, and in others following in this chapter, race does not seem to affect the answers regarding aspirations once sex is controlled. But, since so few migrants have any aspirations, the number of cases becomes too small for adequate analysis. It must be remembered in this chapter, therefore, that more of the women are non-white and hence any differences according to sex may also involve the corresponding racial differences.

that there was an excellent or good chance; 27 per cent thought the chances were average; 23 per cent felt that they had little or no chance; 20 per cent would not estimate their chances, and said they didn't know. The women are less likely (26 per cent) than the men (37 per cent) to think their chances are good; many of them being confined to the household are thus deprived of a chance to work.

Those whose aspirations require more movement within the occupational strata are usually more pessimistic; a total of 34 per cent of the wageworkers and those not now working who aspire to white-collar work think they have little or no chance; but only 12 per cent of those who want to change jobs within the wage-worker stratum, or enter the labor force there, think that they will not be able to do so.

The general poverty of hopefulness among the migrants about achieving occupational aspirations is to some extent anchored in their realization that success up the American occupational ladder depends in large part upon the education one has had. When asked which of four statements best expressed their way of thinking, only 8 per cent chose, "I spent too much time in school," or "I spent enough time in school." Some 40 per cent "should have liked to spend a little more time in school," and 52 per cent "should have liked to spend much more time in school."

Those migrants who have had less than nine years of school are most apt to feel that they need much more; while those who have had at least some high school would have liked to have spent a little more. But more important to the problem of aspiration and its basis in psychological reality is the fact that those men or women who see a good chance to achieve their aspirations feel the lack of adequate schooling as much as those who see little or no chance. No matter how the migrants gauge their chances to achieve their aspirations, at least half of them say that they should have much more schooling, and from 30 to 40 per cent would have liked a little more.

Such answers, reflecting the desire for education irrespective of vocational expectations, may be tied in with an awareness of the socially marginal position the migrants occupy; whether or not they get a different job, whether or not they raise themselves within the wageworker stratum, the Puerto Ricans may feel that they still could not leave the restricted worlds of Spanish Harlem and Morrisiana. To follow the classic pattern of assimilation, an economic transit is not enough; social and cultural mobility is as important. In the American social structure such a pattern is less and less available to those without necessary education. That so many migrants feel their educational lack, which in turn of course confines them to the lower skilled jobs, may indicate that they realize a social ceiling above and beyond any occupational aspirations they might have.

Thus, many migrants cannot or do not articulate an aspiration for a different occupation; and few of those who do feel that their chances are good. As a low-educated, low-skilled group, they are schooled enough in the ways of American social mobility to know that they do not have the necessary education which might allow them to climb the ladder. Of all the migrants interviewed, only 18 per cent of the men, and 10 per cent of the women, articulated a job aspiration of any kind and thought they had a good or excellent chance of realizing it.

3

Although few migrants aspire to a high level job for themselves, an overwhelming number do aspire to white-collar or professional jobs for their children. When asked what occupation they would like to have their children follow,* 81 per cent of the migrants specified certain occupations, 2 per cent said, "what-

---

* This question was asked of all migrants, regardless of whether or not they had any children at all. If they had no children they were asked to say what they would like them to do if they had any. Many migrants who had no children were able to say what they would prefer, hence the 17 per cent who do not answer the question is composed of only small proportions of people with no children.

he chooses," and 17 per cent did not or could not answer the question.

Of those who specified occupations for their children, 71 per cent named white-collar jobs (contrasted to the 32 per cent who prefer such jobs for themselves). Twenty-five per cent would like their children to have skilled jobs; only 3 per cent, semi- or unskilled wagework; and less than 1 per cent specified farm ownership.

Considering the present occupational concentration of the migrants in semi- and unskilled wagework, the low level of their aspirations for themselves, and the amount of pessimism about achieving such aspirations as they do have, it can be seen that the migrants do seem to place their hopes for a future rise in status into the lives of their children.

This major desire of the migrants for their children is constant, regardless of what the migrant's own present job may be; however, those who are unemployed or who are in unskilled jobs are more apt to prefer skilled wageworker jobs for their sons than those who are themselves working on skilled or white-collar levels.

There is a further difference between the aspirations of the migrants for themselves and for their children. When the migrants say that *they* would like to have a white-collar job, they uniformly mean clerical jobs or the ownership of a business; when they say white collar for their sons, they mean professional positions (62 per cent). So, in their aspirations, the Puerto Rican migrants are adapting to the more generalized norms of educated status. If their children did reach such positions, they would reach a respected status in the American community now closed to the migrants themselves. That, it would seem, is the dream of most Puerto Rican migrants.

Yet further evidence indicates that many are as pessimistic about such opportunities for their children as for themselves. When asked the follow-up question: "Regardless of what you hope, what do you think it's most likely that your children will do?" only 35 per cent of the migrants specify a particular occupation; 65 per cent say that they don't know what their children are likely to do.*

This could be due to any one of four factors: (1) the migrants have never thought about the question enough to have any opinions, thus again attesting to a poverty of aspiration; (2) they simply do not know what will happen to their children, thus attesting to the uncertainty about and inability to project into the future; (3) they have considerable doubts as to whether their children will meet their aspirations for them, and are reluctant to express these doubts, thus attesting to a "realistic pessimism"; or (4) their sons are too old, already working in some job, and the possibilities of their obtaining other positions more in line with their parents' aspirations are already closed to them.

These are speculations, of course. That not answering the question may be considered in large part an unhopeful response is further indicated by the types of answers given by those who do say what they think their sons are likely to become. These migrants almost unanimously assert that they expect their sons to do what they would like them to do. Eighty per cent of those who would prefer their children to have white-collar jobs say they think it is likely that they will have them. Sixty-three per cent of those who prefer skilled, and 64 per cent of those who prefer semi- or unskilled jobs, think it is highly possible that their children will have these jobs.

Such a high agreement between aspirations and expectations can arise either because these migrants really are hopeful about their sons' futures or because their sons are already working in the jobs they would prefer—which would mean either a successful realization of their aspirations or an adjustment of aspiration to reality. As very few migrants would like their children to be on the low level of semi- or unskilled wagework, it would seem that those who have adjusted their aspirations represent only a small proportion of those stating their expectations. Any answer to

* Excluded from the base of these percentages are the people without children who are able to say what they would like for them if they had any, but do not answer the question on what they think he would likely have become.

questions about the sons' expected future would thus seem to mean a hopeful attitude toward their aspirations for their children; but the larger proportions, those who refuse to state any expectations seriously, probably doubt the realization of whatever desires they may from time to time entertain.*

Sixty-one per cent of the migrants would like their children to attend college, compared to the 2 per cent of the migrants who have gone to college themselves. Twenty-five per cent limit their educational hopes for their children to high school; only 3 per cent specify the grammar school level or less; and 11 per cent do not answer the question.

TABLE IX-4. PREFERRED OCCUPATION AND PREFERRED
EDUCATIONAL LEVEL FOR CHILDREN

Realistic aspirations		69%
Professional career with college training	48	
Business or clerical career with college or high school training	7	
Wageworker career with high school or grammar school training	14	
Unrealistic aspirations		31%
Professional career with high school or grammar school training	10	
Business or clerical career with grammar school training	*	
Wageworker career with college training	21	
Total having both educational and occupational aspirations for children (100%)		(935)

* Less than 1 per cent.

There is a slight but consistent tendency for migrants with higher educations to want college education for their sons. The migrants are quite realistic in the relation between their educa-

* If we were to make assumptions on this basis, it would mean that roughly one quarter of all the migrants have aspirations for their sons and are hopeful of their realization; that about one half have aspirations and are doubtful; and that one quarter have no articulated occupational aspirations for their sons.

tional aims for their children and the types of occupations they would like to see them enter: 69 per cent aspire to comparable educational and occupational levels for their children.

In so far as the migrants are unrealistic concerning the education needed for the desired occupation, their educational aspirations are higher than the occupational: twice as many prefer college educations while specifying wageworker jobs as prefer higher level jobs without the necessary college training.

In their educational aspirations, as in those of occupation, many of the migrants do not expect their children to achieve the aspirations they hold for them. Twenty-five per cent of the migrants say that they expect their children to have college educations, compared with the 61 per cent who had such aspirations. Forty-one per cent expect no more than high school; 9 per cent, grammar school; and 25 per cent cannot or do not answer the question.*

The cross-classification of aspired and expected education for sons results in the following table.

TABLE IX-5. EXPECTED EDUCATIONAL ATTAINMENT OF CHILDREN, BY PREFERRED EDUCATION

Expected education for children	Preferred education for children		
	College	High school	Grammar school
College	34%	4%	—
High school	35	61	10
Grammar school	5	13	71
No answer	26	22	19
TOTAL[a] (100%)	(688)	(275)	(31)

[a] Excludes 119 cases who do not answer the questions on the *preferred* education for their children.

Only 34 per cent of those who would like their children to go

* That those who do not answer this question may be doubtful about attaining their goals can be seen by the fact that the higher the educational aspiration, the more they are apt to avoid the question by stating no expectations.

to college think that they will do so; while 61 per cent of those who aspire to the high school level, and 71 per cent to the grammar school, expect their sons to fulfill their aspirations for them. The higher the migrants' educational aspirations, the more dreamlike they seem when tempered with expectations.

Some migrants aspire to better jobs for themselves; many more aspire to better jobs and higher educational attainments for their sons; in both cases their expectations that any of these aspirations will be realized are low.

The absence of hopeful aspirations among the migrants is not compensated to any considerable extent by projecting aspirations and expectations to their sons. Those who have low expectations about their own aspirations are no more likely than those with

TABLE IX-6. ASPIRATIONS AND EXPECTATIONS FOR CHILDREN, BY THOSE FOR SELF

	Expectations concerning aspirations for self					Have no aspirations for self
	Good	Av'ge	Low	Don't know	No ans.	
Have aspirations for children	86%	87%	81%	87%	75%	80%
Expectations:						
High	18	21	20	10	12	17
Int.	6	9	7	9	8	8
Low	1	2	3	2	1	1
No answer	61	55	51	66	54	54
Have no aspirations for son or no answer on question for children	14	13	19	13	25	20
TOTAL[a] (100%)	(146)	(86)	(146)	(100)	(74)	(261)

[a] Excludes 300 cases who do not answer the question on their own aspirations.

high personal aspirations to have high expectations for their sons. In fact, those with no aspirations for themselves, or low expectations of achieving what aspirations they have, are less likely than those with high personal expectations, to have any aspirations for their children whatsoever. Both hope and pessimism are transferred along with aspirations to the next generation. Most of the hopeful migrants are hopeful about their children's chances; whereas those who see little chance for themselves are almost as likely to see no chance for their children as to see a good chance. There are no significant differences between men and women on this point.

4

In order to find out the extent to which the migrants' aspirations and expectations for themselves were anchored in active striving, we asked those who said they would like a different occupation, "Are you doing anything now to help you get it?" Twenty-six per cent said that they were doing something towards making such a change; 49 per cent said they were doing nothing, and 25 per cent did not know.

Those who are doing something about realizing their aspirations have the highest expectations about obtaining them. Fifty-one per cent of those who are doing something have such high expectations, while 42 per cent of those who are doing nothing expect that there is little or no chance of achieving their aspiration.

Those who are doing something about their aspirations and think they have a good chance of realizing them, the successful strivers, make up only a small proportion of the migrants: 14 per cent of the men, 4 per cent of the women.

Of only 14 per cent of the men could it be said that they see themselves hopefully as strivers—wanting a change, doing something about it, and feeling that the chances of success are high. Considerable proportions of the migrants, especially among the women (37 per cent) seem to be yearners—they want a change but are doing nothing about obtaining it; whereas, as we have already seen, quite a number have no aspirations for themselves at all.

The aspiring group as a whole, however, cannot be characterized as being any one of these types. The migrants vary con-

TABLE IX-7. ASPIRATIONS, EXPECTATIONS, AND WHETHER OR NOT MIGRANTS
ARE DOING ANYTHING ABOUT THEM

	Men	Women
Have occupational aspirations for themselves *and* are *doing something about them*	28%	6%
Expectations of obtaining them		
Good	14	4
Average	6	2
Poor	4	*
No answer or		
don't know	4	*
Have occupational aspirations for themselves *and are* not *doing anything about them*ᵃ	22%	37%
Expectations of obtaining them		
Good	4	6
Average	3	5
Poor	11	13
No answer or		
don't know	4	13
*Have no occupational aspirations*ᵇ	50%	57%
TOTAL (100%)	(417)	(696)

* Less than 1 per cent.
ᵃ Includes "Don't Know" and no answer on "are you doing anything to get it."
ᵇ Includes those who do not answer the question on whether or not they have aspirations.

siderably in their aspirations, expectations, and activities; no one pattern can be found that is truly representative of them. This very lack of any general pattern is, in fact, a distinctive aspect of their present condition.

5

The willful feeling that the individual can command the future to serve his own ends may be historically characteristic of industrial Protestant culture, but it is not a signal feature of the Latin American. However much this feeling may have diminished recently in America, it is still a principle guideline by which Americans sight their aspirations and plans for the future. Latin American conditions of life have not encouraged this kind of ambitious focussing upon one's future and willful searching for the means of achieving it. The Puerto Ricans in New York City, in the quality and connections of their dream life, are again caught between two conflicting cultures; some few have begun planfully to strive but most retain the heritage of their island background.

This background is further buttressed in New York by limited job mobility, which sometimes actually entails a downward movement from Puerto Rico to New York. The petty defeats Puerto Ricans continually face may cut the nerve of that kind of straining into the future which characterizes aspiration.

Moreover, the Puerto Rican population of New York City's core areas seems to be a fairly homogeneous group. Differences do arise in age, sex, color, and time of migration, but on the whole there is rather uniform educational achievement, standardized occupation in specific industries and in standardized areas of the city. These factors of institutional concentration which tend to make the migrants of Spanish Harlem and Morrisania homogeneous have more effect than certain other factors which tend to differentiate between them; the over-all result is a leveling of psychological and internal life.

There are, after all, no genuinely spontaneous community organizations among the migrants that would differentiate them from other elements of the lower-class mass of the metropolis. They are exposed to many common experiences which reinforce the lack of positional difference among them. By living at a similar class level, in the same regions of the city, doing the same type of work, having the same type of troubles, being exposed to the same type of mass communications, their imaginative life becomes leveled out. In their day-to-day struggle, absorbed in the need to function inconspicuously with a minimum of psychic discomfort, they have little time left over for thought about the future.

Notes and Sources

1. E. B. Reuter, "Culture Contacts in Puerto Rico," *American Journal of Sociology*, LII (September, 1946), p. 95.

2. Antonio S. Pedreira, *Insularismo*, San Juan, "Biblioteca de Autores Puertoriquenos," 1946, pp. 168-74. *Informe sobre el Censo de Puerto Rico*, 1899, Washington. Imprenta del Gobierno, 1900, pp. 78, 82, 117. Henry K. Carroll, *Report on the Island of Puerto Rico* (Washington: Government Printing Office, 1899), 813 pp.

3. U.S. Department of Agriculture, *Trade of Puerto Rico*, 1898, cited in Sol. L. Descartes, *Basic Statistics on Puerto Rico* (Washington: Office of Puerto Rico, 1946), p. 49.

4. Salvador Brau, *La Colonización de Puerto Rico*, San Juan, Tipografía, "Heraldo Español," 1907, pp. 412-14. Brau, after analyzing various reports, comes to the conclusion that there were probably only around 16,000 Indians inhabiting the island when the Spaniards arrived, instead of the 600,000 sometimes claimed, and that in two and a half centuries their numbers had been reduced by about nine-tenths. The 1777 census showed 1756 not crossed with either whites or Negroes. By 1808 the authorities dropped the designation "indian" from their nomenclature.

5. The figures for 1899 are from *Census of Puerto Rico, 1899*, p. 57. The figures for 1940 are from *16th Census of the United States, Puerto Rico, Population*, Bulletin 2, p. 8. All other following information as of 1899 or 1940 are from the same sources, unless otherwise noted.

6. Pablo Morales Otero, and Manuel Perez, *Health and Socio-Economic Studies in Puerto Rico* (San Juan: School of Tropical Medicine, 1941), pp. 56, 256.

7. For a psychiatric treatment of the situation, see Renzo Sereno,

"Cryptomelanism: A Study of Color Relations and Personal Insecurity in Puerto Rico," *Psychiatry*, X (August, 1947), pp. 261-69.

8. Department of Commerce and Agriculture, *Annual Book on Statistics of Puerto Rico* (San Juan, 1948), p. 11.

9. Morris Siegel, unpublished ms. of a study under the auspices of the Social Science Research Center, University of Puerto Rico, p. 112.

10. Pablo Morales Otero, and Manuel Perez, *op. cit.*, pp. 76 & 254.

11. Ismael Rodriquez Bou, *Para Ver, Pensar y Actuar*, Rio Piedras, Consejo Superior de Enseñanza, 1942, p. 28.

12. Taken from various sections of the 1945–46 *Report of the Commissioner of Education*, San Juan, 1946.

13. Mariano Villaronga, "The Teaching of English in Puerto Rico," San Juan, Department of Education, 1947, p. 75 (mimeo).

14. U. S. Census, 1940, Puerto Rico, *Population*, Bulletin 2, p. 14. It is instructive to compare this figure with that for the United States as a whole in 1940, in which only 25 per cent of the population was less than 15 years of age. This helps explain why more children are without schools now than 48 years ago: 288,000 in 1900; 310,000 in 1945–46. See *Annual Report of Commissioner of Education*, 1945–46, and Jaime Benitez, *Democracy and Education in Puerto Rico* (Washington: Office of Puerto Rico, 1947), p. 5.

15. Letter from Commissioner Mariano Villaronga, March 30, 1949.

16. *Universidad* (Rio Piedras, febrero, 1949), p. 1.

17. The island sends an elected resident commissioner to Congress. His responsibility is to present the Puerto Rican point of view. He has no congressional vote.

18. President Truman appointed the Hon. Jesús T. Pinero, the first Puerto Rican to serve as governor, in 1946. Congress in August, 1947, amended the Organic Act of Puerto Rico to allow the popular election of governor. The first such election was held in November, 1948. The governor is now empowered to appoint his own cabinet members, except for the auditor. Supreme Court judges will continue to be appointed by the President of the United States.

19. Jaime Benitiz, *op. cit.*, p. 14.

20. The scope of these activities is indicated in this list of agencies which are active on the island. Most of them have been created since 1940.

Agriculture Development Co.
Aqueduct & Sewerage Service
Civil Service Commission
Coffee Insurance Corporation
Development Bank
Industrial Development Co.
Labor Relations Board
Land Authority
Minimum Wage Board
Office of Industrial Tax Exemption
Planning, Zoning and Urbanizing Board
Public Recreation and Park Commission

P. R. Clay Products Corp.
P. R. Communications Authority
P. R. Glass Corp.
P. R. Housing Authority
P. R. Pulp and Paper Corp.
P. R. Shoe & Leather Corp.
P. R. Transportation Authority
P. R. Water Resources Authority
School of Industrial Arts
School of Public Administration
Social Science Research Center
Telares de Puerto Rico, Inc.
Tobacco Institute

21. Puerto Rico Planning Board, *A Development Plan for Puerto Rico* (Santurce, 1944), p. 18.

22. Harvey S. Perloff, *Puerto Rico's Economic Future* (Chicago: Univ. of Chicago Press, 1950), p. 55.

23. Sol L. Descartes, *Basic Statistics on Puerto Rico* (Washington: Office of Puerto Rico, 1946), p. 50.

24. *Ley de Tierras* (San Juan: Autoridad de Tierras, 1942), p. 6.

25. See Walter E. Packard, "The Land Authority and Democratic Processes in Puerto Rico," *Inter-American Economic Affairs* (Summer, 1948), pp. 49-101. (Reprint available from Editorial Universitaria, Rio Piedras, Puerto Rico.)

26. Perloff, *op. cit.*, Appendix B.

27. *Loc. cit.*

28. Daniel Creamer, *The Net Income of the Puerto Rican Economy, 1940–44.* (Rio Piedras: Social Science Research Center, 1947), p. 23, for the 1939–44 data; the preliminary figures are taken from Puerto Rico's exhibit #13 in Civil Aeronautics Board, *Docket* #3341, Washington, 1949.

29. Perloff, *op. cit.*, pp. 87-88.

30. *The Economic Review*, San Juan (June, 1945).

PUERTO RICO COMPARED WITH OTHER CARIBBEAN AREAS
(1941–1944 PER CAPITA AVERAGES)

Per capita (or as noted)	Puerto Rico	Dominican Republic	Haiti	Cuba	Jamaica	Trinidad	Barbados
National income (Net individual earnings)	$183.00	$ 63.00	$24.00	$129.00	$108.00	$143.00	$117.00
Gross wealth	$317.00	$109.00	$33.00	$199.00	$145.00	$236.00	$183.00
Gov't. expenditures for education	$ 6.34	$ 1.61	$ 0.40	$ 3.72	$ 1.13	$ 2.34	$ 2.02
Gov't. expenditures for public health	$ 3.93	$ 0.76	$ 0.26	$ 1.65	$ 0.54	$ 2.63	$ 1.44
Motor vehicles per 1,000 population	14	1.8	0.6	5.7	3.9	7	4.2
Radios per 1,000 population	43	10.8	2.8	27	24	29	12
Clothing purchases at wholesale prices	$ 18.90	$ 5.64	$ 2.72	$ 8.94	$ 6.41	$ 10.67	$ 6.65
Silk hosiery purchases per female inhabitant	1.42	.08	.02	.32	.15	.43	.21
Motion pictures	3.76	.32	.11	2.21	.98	1.35	.72
Government revenue	77.00	9.00	2.00	21.00	14.00	43.00	15.00

Dollar ranks must, of course, be adjusted for price levels and amount of home-produced commodities. The dollar comparisons are given, however, even though they are not strictly comparable, since the variation, especially among the more industrialized countries, is felt to be less than the variation between the dollar values. The 1943–44 per capita income for Puerto Rico was $239. Only seven countries showed per capita incomes in the early 1940's of over $100: Argentina, $182; Brazil, $109; Chile, $106; Costa Rica, $134; Cuba, $129; and Venezuela, $200. Others ran: Ecuador, $34; El Salvador, $55; Honduras, $58; Mexico, $84; Paraguay, $20; and Peru, $62. Source: "Basic Economic Data Concerning the 20 Latin American Republics," in George Wythe, *An Outline of Latin American Economic Development* (New York: Barnes and Noble, 1946), pp. 244–45.

31.

RATES OF BIRTH, DEATH, & NATURAL INCREASE (PER 1,000)[a]

Date	Birth rate	Death rate	Rate of Natural increase
1900–04 (Annual average)	38.0	27.1	10.9
1910	40.4	24.0	16.4
1920	39.3	22.1	17.2
1930	39.0	20.1	18.9
1940	38.7	18.4	20.3
1945	42.3	14.1	28.2
1947	45.8	12.5	31.3

[a] The rate of natural increase for the United States as a whole was as follows: 1920, 10.7; 1930, 7.6; and 1940, 7.1. The rate for New York State in 1940 was 3.5. Other countries, in the immediate prewar years showed such rates as: Russia, 23.2; India, 11.5; Japan, 12.5; Egypt, 16.0; Jamaica, 15.7; the Philippines, 15.4; Germany, 7.5; and Italy, 9.3.

Source: Frederick P. Bartlett, and Brandon Howell, *Puerto Rico y su problema de poblacion* (Santurce: 1946), p. 62; Sol L. Descartes, *Basic Statistics on Puerto Rico* (Washington: 1946), p. 11; *Report of the Commissioner of Health* (San Juan: 1947), p. 8.

32. Henry K. Carroll, *op. cit.*, pp. 212-16; Garver and Fincher, *Puerto Rico, Unsolved Problem* (Elgin, Ill.: The Elgin Press, 1945), p. 71.

33. *Report of the Commissioner of Health*, San Juan, 1937–38, p. 96; *Monthly Statistical Report*, San Juan (Oct.–Nov., 1947), p. 29; Division of Statistics Report, March 7, 1950.

34. Life tables compiled by Jose Janer, "Population Growth in Puerto Rico and Its Relation to Time Changes in Vital Statistics," *Human Biology*, Vol. 17 (December, 1945), pp. 285, 288, show that the life expectation of the white population of the continental United States in 1940 was 18 years greater for males and 20 years greater for females; that of the Negro population was 8 years greater.

35. Lydia J. Roberts, unpublished study made in the summer of 1946 for the Social Science Research Center, University of Puerto Rico. This study reported on a sample of 443 urban households. The ratio of stillbirths to live births among urban mothers whose income was less than $200 was 43.1 per cent. In the $3000 and over income

class the ratio was 8.4 per cent. Rural households showed almost the same ratio, although the rates were lower at both ends of the income scale: 25.8 per cent for those under $200 and 5.8 per cent in the $3000 and over class.

36. Ana Teresa Blanco, *Nutrition Studies in Puerto Rico* (Rio Piedras: Social Science Research Center, University of Puerto Rico,

FOOD CONSUMPTION IN PUERTO RICO: RECOMMENDED AND ACTUAL

Food group	N. R.P.B. per capita requirements, lbs. per year[a]	B.H.N.H.E. low-cost adequate diet, lbs. per year[b]	Actual consumption as shown by wage-earner study, lbs. per week ✕ 52[c]
Milk and dairy products except butter[d]	581	522	153
Potatoes, other starchy vegetables, fruit (except citrus)	338	332	418
Dried beans, peas, nuts	28	35	63
Citrus fruits, tomatoes	81	74	25
Leafy green and yellow vegetables	102	65	6
Eggs	23	19	8
Lean meat, poultry, fish	73	45	41
Flour, cereals (including rice)[e]	190	160	215
Fats and oils (including salt pork)	47	34	36
Sugars	47	43	60
	1510	1329	1025

[a] National Resources Planning Board, "Minimum Decent Living Standards for Puerto Rico," San Juan, December, 1942.

[b] Diet plan developed by the Bureau of Human Nutrition and Home Economics, Department of Agriculture, for use in Puerto Rico in 1941 at the request of the Farm Security Administration.

[c] Survey of Incomes and Expenditures of Wage Earners in Puerto Rico, 1941–42.

[d] Milk and dairy products converted to equivalent whole milk.

[e] Bread and crackers converted to flour equivalent.

Source: Alice C. Hanson, and Manuel ·A. Perez, "Incomes and Expenditures of Wage Earners in Puerto Rico," Dept. of Labor, Government of Puerto Rico, Bulletin No. 1, May 1, 1947.

1946), p. 88; Pablo Morales Otero, "Puerto Rican Nutritional Problems," *Boletin de la Oficina Sanitaria Panamericana* (marzo, 1946), p. 233. Food consumption is as shown in the table above, with a comparison between the actual consumption and that recommended by two government agencies.

37.

MORBIDITY RATES BY LEADING CAUSES, 1936 AND 1946
(PER 100,000 POPULATION)

Cause of illness	1936	1946
Typhoid	60.5	8.5
Diphtheria	37.2	27.7
Malaria	849.2	268.5
Tuberculosis (all forms)	612.5	303.8
Influenza	81.3	69.0
Dysentery	35.8	100.6
Syphilis	35.6	383.1
Gonorrhea	a	285.2

ᵃ Not available.

Source: Letter from Bureau of Registry and Vital Statistics, Puerto Rican Department of Health.

Two comments on these figures should be made. First, the dysentery rate jumped in 1946 to about five times its 1935–45 rate, which was 18.4. Second, the venereal disease rate reflects two phenomena: the war, which brought an increase everywhere in the world where there were numbers of troops, sailors, and merchant seamen; and the increased effectiveness of educational campaigns bringing infected persons to medical centers.

38. For a survey of the program see Thomas Hibben, and Rafael Pico, *Industrial Development of Puerto Rico and the Virgin Islands* (Port-of-Spain, Trinidad, B.W.I.: Caribbean Commission, 1948), pp. 1-268.

39. These possibilities are discussed in Carmen R. de Alvarado, and Christopher Tietze, "Birth Control in Puerto Rico," *Human Fertility* (March, 1947), pp. 15-18; Christopher Tietze, "Human Fertility in Puerto Rico," *American Journal of Sociology* (July, 1947), pp. 34-40; and Clarence Senior, "Population Pressures and

PUERTO RICAN DEATH RATES BY LEADING CAUSES,
1936 AND 1946 (PER 100,000 POPULATION)

Cause of illness	1936	1946
Diarrhea and enteritis (all ages)	488.2	225.9
Tuberculosis (all forms)	305.3	207.6
Pneumonia (all forms)	161.9	116.2
Diseases of the heart	114.0	99.7
Malaria	141.1	32.3
Nephritis	125.1	55.5
Cancer	52.0	48.4
Diseases of pregnancy, childbirth, and the puerperium[a]	51.8	26.7
Accidents	35.0	29.3
Diseases of the Arteries	31.3	16.8
Cerebral hemorrhage, embolism, Thrombosis, hemiplegia, etc.	24.3	30.6
Suicides	31.5	25.5
Anemia	24.4	14.3
Bronchitis	35.5	17.5
Syphilis	32.2	9.9
Homicides	19.1	14.7
Uncinariasis	13.8	2.2
Whooping cough	5.0	6.7
Influenza	47.7	11.0

[a] Rates computed per 10,000 total births.
Source: Annual Reports of the Commissioner of Health of Puerto Rico, 1937–38 and 1947–48.

the Future of Puerto Rico," *Journal of Heredity* (May, 1947), pp. 130-134 and *Puerto Rico Emigration*, (Rio Piedras: Social Science Research Council, 1947). See also Julius Isaac, *Economics of Migration* (New York: Oxford University Press, 1947).

40. Between 1925 and 1940, 108,293 persons, or 5.8 per cent of the population, moved from one municipio (county) to another. In the same five-year period, 54 of the 77 municipalities lost population. Calculations for the 1930–40 decade show that 61 municipalities lost people; 33 lost 10 per cent or more of their 1930 population and six lost 20 per cent or more.

Urban centers (over 2500) accounted in 1940 for 30.3 per cent of the population compared with 27.7 per cent in 1930, 21.8 per cent in 1920, and 14.6 per cent in 1899. San Juan increased its numbers by 47.6 per cent from 1930 to 1940; Rio Piedras, 67.2; Guaynabo, 35.7; Mayaguez, 31.2; and Arroyo, 31, but the total population increased only 21.1 per cent (U. S. Census, 1940, Puerto Rico, *Population*, Bulletin No. 4). The effect of the urbanization trend is shown by the differential fertility rates. The number of children under 5 years of age per 1,000 women of child-bearing age in the open country in 1940 was almost exactly double the number in San Juan: 731 against 365. There is a steady increase as urbanization decreases. Cities of the 10-to-20,000 class show 411; rural towns, 507. Christopher Tietze, "Human Fertility in Puerto Rico," *American Journal of Sociology* (July, 1947), pp. 34-40.

CHAPTER 2

1. Published estimates of the number of Puerto Ricans in New York City in the middle and later Forties have ranged from 210,000 to 710,000! On the basis of our field work in the two core areas (an enumeration of every tenth household, giving information enabling us to determine the average size of, and the average number of children in, the Puerto Rican households visited), we have been able to revise and project (1) school data on the number of Puerto Rican children in public schools and the Welfare Council Committee's estimate of the number of Puerto Rican children in parochial schools, (2) welfare data on the number of Puerto Ricans in the various districts of the city, and (3) 1940 census data, combined with subsequent migration data, into three separate estimates, one for each of these sources, of the number of Puerto Ricans in New York City. The close resemblance of the estimates based on these revisions and projections leads us to believe that, in the early part of 1948, the number of Puerto Ricans in New York City probably was in the neighborhood of 200,000.

2. These sex ratios are computed for sample members 18 years old and over; for islanders 20 years old and over. (See Appendix II: The Sample.) The sex ratio for the island as a whole and for urban areas is found in U. S. Census, 1940, Puerto Rico, *Population*, Bulletin 2, p. 8.

3.

SEX RATIO (MEN PER 100 WOMEN) OF ALL PUERTO RICAN MIGRANTS TO SPANISH HARLEM AND MORRISANIA BY COLOR AND TIME OF ARRIVAL

Time of arrival	White men per 100 white women	Intermediate men per 100 intermediate women	Negro men per 100 Negro women	All men per 100 women
Postwar years (1946 to spring, 1948)	68	49	88	68
War years (1942–1945)	74	65	41	65
Prewar years	65	42	26	52
1930–1941	46	37	22	40
1920–1929	90	50	30	68
Combined index	70	49	41	63

4.

RATE OF ENTRY INTO SPANISH HARLEM AND MORRISANIA BY SEX AND RACE (1920–29=100)

Year of migration	Men				Women			
	White	Intermediate	Negro	All men	White	Intermediate	Negro	All women
1947	360	550	430	383	480	1100	234	490
1946	340	1100	1650	575	450	590	470	474
1945	180	450	430	270	350	410	280	343
1942–44	103	330	143	154	140	214	107	140
1940–41	83	180	72	92	205	68	96	157
1930–39	53	64	57	66	96	123	77	112
1920–29	100	100	100	100	100	100	100	100

5. U. S. Census, 1940, Puerto Rico, *Population*, Bulletin 2, pp. 11-14.

6. T. Lynn Smith, *Population Analysis* (New York: McGraw-Hill), p. 261.

7.

MARITAL STATUS OF PUERTO RICAN MIGRANTS COMPARED WITH ADULT ISLANDERS, BY SEX (PERCENTAGES)

| | Migrants: 1947 | | | | | | Puerto Rican Adults, 1940[a] | |
| | White | | Colored | | All | | | |
Marital status	Men	Women	Men	Women	Men	Women	Men	Women
Single	13%	10%	16%	9%	14%	10%	42%	31%
Legal marriage	78	58	69	53	75	56	39	40
Consensual marriage	4	1	7	7	5	4	14	15
Legal marriage broken by divorce or desertion	4	16	4	16	4	16	1	6
Legal marriage broken by death	1	11	3	11	2	11	4	8
Consensual marriage broken by death or desertion	*	4	1	4	*	3	—	—
TOTAL (100%)	(293)	(418)	(122)	(277)	(415)	(695)	(554)[b]	(556)[b]

[a] Fifteen years of age and over.
[b] In thousands.
* Less than one per cent.
Source of Insular data: U. S. Census, 1940, Puerto Rico, *Population*, Bulletin 2, p. 18, except the fourth and sixth categories. Data in the fourth are from the references cited in Table II-5. We found no comparable data for Puerto Rico in the sixth.

8. U. S. Census, 1940, Puerto Rico, *Population*, Bulletin 2, p. 70.

9. The New York figures are taken from a report released by the New York Adult Education Council, as reported in the *New York Times*, January 9, 1949.

10.

EDUCATIONAL LEVEL OF PUERTO RICAN MALE AND FEMALE MIGRANTS IN
NEW YORK CITY'S TWO CORE AREAS

	Male			Female		
Education	White	Colored	Total	White	Colored	Total
None	2%	8%	4%	11%	12 %	11%
1–5 years grade school	26	33	28	30	43	35
6–8 years grade school	40	34	38	32	27	30
High school	29	22	27	26	17	23
College	3	3	3	1	1	1
TOTAL (100%)	(290)	(121)	(413)	(416)	(274)	(691)

11. U. S. Census, 1940, Puerto Rico, *Population*, Bulletin 2, pp. 8-9.

12.

LAST RESIDENCE OF MIGRANTS ON THE ISLAND BY SEX, COLOR, AND TIME OF ARRIVAL

	Men						Women					
	White		Colored		Both		White		Colored		Both	
Island Residence	Re-cent	Ear-ly	Re-cent	Ear-ly	Re-cent	Ear-ly	Re-cent	Ear-ly	Re-cent	Ear-ly	Re-cent	Ear-ly
Rural	8%	5%	11%	3%	10%	5%	16%	9%	9%	5%	13%	7%
Urban	92	95	89	97	90	95	84	91	91	95	87	93
TOTAL (100%)	(122)	(171)	(74)	(48)	(196)	(219)	(173)	(245)	(124)	(153)	(297)	(398)

13.

LAST RESIDENCE IN PUERTO RICO OF MIGRANTS COMPARED WITH DISTRIBUTION OF ISLAND POPULATION IN 1940

	Migrants	Islanders[a]
San Juan	50%	30%
Ponce	20	20
Mayaguez	12	11
Caguas	8	16
Humacao	4	7
Adjuntas	3	10
Aguadilla	3	6
TOTAL (100%)	(1113)	(1,869,255)

[a] Source: U. S. Census, 1940, Puerto Rico, *Population*, Bulletin 1, p. 3.

14.

LAST RESIDENCE IN PUERTO RICO OF MIGRANTS BY SEX AND COLOR

Last residence (census district)	Men				Women			
	Recent		Early		Recent		Early	
	White	Colored	White	Colored	White	Colored	White	Colored
San Juan	53%	59%	41%	56%	47%	59%	44%	55%
Ponce	15	15	21	12	15	14	25	26
Mayaguez	13	7	15	16	18	11	25	26
Caguas	10	8	10	4	10	6	12	11
Humacao	2	11	3	8	4	8	8	4
Adjuntas	2	—	5	4	4	1	4	3
Aguadilla	5	—	5	—	2	1	3	1
TOTAL (100%)	(122)	(74)	(171)	(48)	(173)	(124)	(245)	(153)

15.

INDUSTRIAL SOURCE OF EMPLOYMENT IN PUERTO RICO
OF MIGRANTS COMPARED WITH ISLAND WORKING
POPULATION IN 1947

	Migrants	Islanders[a]
Agriculture	5%	39%
Manufacturing and processing	47	24
Trade and trans.	15	17
Service	33	20
TOTAL (100%)	(608)	(200,023)

[a] Source: Perloff, *op. cit.*, p. 55.

16. On the Island as a whole, in 1940, 79.4 per cent of the men
and 25 per cent of the women over 14 were in the labor force.
Source: U. S. Census, 1940, Puerto Rico, *Population*, Bulletin 2,
pp. 24-25.

17. Source: Sol Descartes, *Basic Statistics on Puerto Rico* (Washington: Office of Puerto Rico, 1946), p. 61; Department of Agriculture & Commerce, *Annual Book on Statistics of Puerto Rico* (San
Juan: 1948), pp. 18-19.

18. For Island figures see U. S. Census, 1940, Puerto Rico, *Population*, Bulletin 3, pp. 54-59.

19. Wage data for the Island as a whole are not available in annual series, for year-by-year comparison between the migrants and
the islanders. The figures cited are estimates based on data received
from the Insular Bureau of Labor Statistics in a letter dated January
15, 1949. The latest figures for wages and salaries in manufacturing
are for March, 1947. See Jornales y Horas Trabajadas en los Indus-
trias de Puerto Rico, Marzo, 1947 (San Juan, Departamento del
Trabajo, 1948). (mimeo.)

20. See Rexford G. Tugwell, *The Stricken Land* (New York:
Doubleday, 1947), *passim* for an account of the war years; Thomas
Hibben, and Rafael Picó, *op. cit.*, p. 105; Governor's Office, *A Re-
port on Unemployment in Puerto Rico in 1942* (San Juan, 1943).

CHAPTER 3

1. The correlation was established between the Babson Statistical Organization's Index of Physical Volume of Business Activity and the flow of migrants as reported by the Immigration and Naturalization Service, and given in Note 2 below. It is interesting to note that this comes close to the correlation found by Thomas between business conditions in the United States and immigration received from the United Kingdom during the period 1870 to 1913, which was .77. See Dorothy S. Thomas, *Social Aspects of the Business Cycle* (London: 1925), p. 151.

2.

BALANCE OF OUT-MIGRATION AND IN-MIGRATION, PUERTO RICO
1908–09 TO 1947–48 (FISCAL YEARS)

Fiscal year	Gain	Loss	Fiscal year	Gain	Loss
1908–09	3111		1928–29		4637
1909–10	3500		1929–30		5676
1910–11	1475		1930–31	1938	
1911–12	195		1931–32	2708	
1912–13	22		1932–33	1082	
1913–14		588	1933–34	2966	
1914–15		339	1934–35		1017
1915–16	33		1935–36		3448
1916–17		2354	1936–37		4518
1917–18		4212	1937–38		2362
1918–19		3312	1938–39		4488
1919–20		4139	1939–40		1904
1920–21	612		1940–41		988
1921–22	633		1941–42		1837
1922–23		1756	1942–43		2599
1923–24		3720	1943–44		7548
1924–25		2137	1944–45		14794
1925–26		5621	1945–46		21631
1926–27		8729	1946–47		34405
1927–28		6144	1947–48		28031
			TOTAL	18,275	182,934
			NET OUT-MIGRATION	164,659	

Source: Clarence Senior, *Puerto Rican Emigration*, Social Science Research Center, University of Puerto Rico. Based on Table III, p. 3.

3. The authors have heard rumors of a $25 fare, but the lowest one seen announced in travel agency windows was $35. The Puerto Rican government's view of what had during the war been a monopoly of air service to the island by Pan American Airways is told in Civil Aeronautics Board, Docket #3341, Exhibits 28-41.

4. See Note 2 above.

5. Harry Jerome, *Migration and Business Cycles* (New York: National Bureau of Economic Research, 1926), Chs. IV-VIII; for later data see *Economic Aspects of Immigration* (New York: National Committee on Immigration Policy, 1947), especially pp. 44-45; and A. R. Eckler and J. Zlotnick, "Immigration and the Labor Force," *Annals* (March, 1949), pp. 92-101.

6. Two other questions were asked in order to verify and further clarify the answers to the question quoted above on New York and Puerto Rico, but the answers only confirmed the results obtained in the original question.

7

SOURCE OF INFORMATION ABOUT NEW YORK, BY LEADERSHIP, AND WHETHER INFORMATION WAS FROM FAMILY OR FRIENDS

| | | *Conversation* | |
	Letters	*What people told you*	*What you asked people*
Deciders			
Yes	67%	78%	43%
Family	52	25	9
Friends	15	53	34
No	33	22	57
TOTAL DECIDERS[a] (100%)	(528)	(528)	(528)
Followers			
Yes	82%	69%	30%
Family	75	32	11
Friends	7	37	19
No	12	21	70
TOTAL FOLLOWERS[b] (100%)	(360)	(360)	(360)

[a] Excludes 4 cases who did not report on sources of information.
[b] Excludes 10 cases who did not report on sources of information.

8.

PUERTO RICANS (BORN IN PUERTO RICO) IN UNITED STATES CITIES OF
OVER 100,000—1910, 1920, AND 1940

	1910	1920	1940
New York City, N. Y.	554	7364	61,463
San Francisco, Calif.	213	474	603
Philadelphia, Pa.	64	319	440
Washington, D. C.	48	148	327
Chicago, Ill.	15	110	240
Baltimore, Md.	44	91	231
Los Angeles, Calif.	10	101	212
Oakland, Calif.	10	101	194
New Orleans, La.	15	177	153
Detroit, Mich.	4	59	153
Newark, N. J.	5	2	146
Tampa, Fla.	0	94	123
Jersey City, N. J.	3	56	106
Boston, Mass.	10	67	91
Buffalo, N. Y.	12	56	62
Cleveland, Ohio	3	26	61
Yonkers, N. Y.	1	13	55
San Antonio, Tex.	6	6	53
Houston, Tex.	0	3	50
St. Louis, Mo.	6	59	50

Sources: Compiled from the Population Volumes of the 13th, 14th, and 16th Censuses
of the United States.

CHAPTER 4

1.

ECONOMIC EXPECTATIONS OF THE MIGRANTS IN COMING TO NEW YORK, BY SEX

Expected employment status in New York	Men	Women	Total
To enter labor force	83%	63%	72%
Not to enter labor force	17	37	28
Housewife[a]	—	20	13
Too young or in school	12	13	13
Ill	—	—	—
Retired	—	—	*
Other	5	4	2
TOTAL[b] (100%)	(417)	(669)	(1086)

* Less than one per cent.
[a] Includes working for board.
[b] Excludes 27 women who did not answer the question.

2.

JOB EXPECTATION IN NEW YORK OF MIGRANTS PLANNING TO ENTER THE NEW YORK LABOR FORCE, BY SEX AND RACE

Job expectation in New York	Men				Women			
	White	Int.	Negro	All	White	Int.	Negro	All
To find any work	66%	69%	53%	65%	65%	85%	78%	71%
To find some special kind of work	22	21	32	23	19	9	16	17
To open own business	2	—	3	2	2	2	1	2
To work and study	8	8	12	8	11	4	3	8
Job lined up in advance	2	2	—	2	3	—	2	2
TOTAL[a] (100%)	(249)	(48)	(52)	(349)	(251)	(69)	(97)	(417)

[a] Includes only those who planned to enter N. Y. labor force.

3.

WHETHER OR NOT THE MIGRANTS EVER ENTERED THE NEW YORK LABOR
FORCE, BY THEIR LABOR FORCE STATUS IN PUERTO RICO AND SEX

Status in New York	Men Status in Puerto Rico		Women Status in Puerto Rico	
	In labor force	Not in lf	In labor force	Not in lf
In labor force	95%[2]	90%[1]	82%	73%
Not in labor force	5[3]	10[4]	18	27
TOTAL (100%)	(300)	(62)	(318)	(322)

4. For each sex group, the four cells of the table above (Note 3)
were classified as 1, entered labor force; 2, always in labor force;
3, left labor force; and 4, never in labor force. In the tables following
in the text showing movement in and out of the labor force between
different time periods, the cells were reduced in the same manner.

5.

INDUSTRIAL HISTORY OF THE MIGRANTS: COMPARISON OF LAST INDUSTRY IN
PUERTO RICO, FIRST INDUSTRY IN NEW YORK, AND PRESENT INDUSTRY IN
NEW YORK

Industrial group	Last job in Puerto Rico	First job in New York	Present job in New York
Manufacturing and processing	47%	61%	56%
Service trades and domestic service	20	30	32
Retail and wholesale trades	13	2	3
Transportation and shipping	2	2	3
Professional service	3	1	3
Government and military	9	3	3
Home industry	1	1	*
Agriculture	5	—	—
TOTAL EMPLOYED (100%)	(609)	(900)	(553)

* Less than one per cent.

6. Each case was classified as experiencing mobility upward (1), stable (2), and downward (3) in the following manner:

First job in New York	Occupation in Puerto Rico				
	White collar*	Skilled	Semi-skilled	Un-skilled—urban and rural	Un-employed—seeking work
White collar**	2	1	1	1	1
Skilled	3	2	1	1	1
Semiskilled	3	3	2	1	1
Unskilled—urban	3	3	3	2	1
Unemployed—seeking work	3	3	3	3	2

* White collar includes professional, small business or farm owners, and clerical workers.
** Does not include any farm owners.

The tables following in the text describing the respondent's occupational mobility between other jobs were reduced in the same manner.

7. Upward (1), stable (2), and downward (3) mobility from father's occupation to migrant's occupation before leaving Puerto Rico was established in the following manner:

Migrant's last job in Puerto Rico	Father's occupation			
	White collar*	Skilled	Semiskilled	Unskilled—urban or rural
White collar*	2	1	1	1
Skilled	3	2	1	1
Semiskilled	3	3	2	1
Unskilled—urban or rural	3	3	3	2

* Includes professional, small business or farm owners and clerical workers.

8. Although we have the raw data, it is not possible to present reliable mobility figures from the migrants' fathers' occupation to

their own present occupation in New York. First, the relative positions of occupations on the island when the migrants were children and those they now hold in New York are not readily comparable. Second, there are many cases for which we have no information on the father's occupation; and thus the problem of getting continuous occupational histories for both father's occupation and those respondents who were in the labor force from the time they left Puerto Rico to now becomes difficult; any results obtained from this data cannot be statistically significant.

Such inconclusive data as we have, however, would seem to indicate that most respondents have either risen above or fallen below the level of their father's occupation; only small proportions have remained stable. Those who have risen are most likely those who rose above their father while still in Puerto Rico. Those who have gone downward from their fathers are those who sank either in Puerto Rico before they came to New York and who, once in New York, were stable; or those who were stable in Puerto Rico, but sank once in New York. Very few cases seem to have suffered a cumulative decline—down from father in Puerto Rico and down from Puerto Rican job to New York position. The reason for this is apparent in the generally low skill levels in which the migrants are concentrated, both in New York and in Puerto Rico.

9.

INCOME HISTORY OF EMPLOYED MIGRANTS: EARNINGS FOR TWO CONSECUTIVE JOBS IN NEW YORK, FIRST JOB IN NEW YORK, AND THREE CONSECUTIVE JOBS IN PUERTO RICO

	New York			Puerto Rico		
Earnings per week	Present job	Before that	First job	Last job in Puerto Rico	Before that	Before that
Under $20	5%	13%	34%	74%	77%	82%
$20–$29	18	29	31	13	12	10
$30–39	37	29	23	9	7	6
$40–$49	20	16	8	3	2	2
$50 and more	20	13	4	1	2	—
TOTAL (100%)	(607)	(451)	(729)	(636)	(234)	(94)

CHAPTER 5

1. Maurice R. Davie, *World Immigration* (New York: 1936), pp. 13-14.

2. U. S. Immigration & Naturalization Service, *Annual Report for 1945.*

3. National Committee on Immigration Policy, *Immigration and Population Policy* (New York: 1947), p. 33.

4. Jack Lait, and Lee Mortimer, *N. Y. Confidential* (Chicago: Ziff Davis, 1948), pp. 126-132.

5. *New York Times*, April 31, 1947.

6. *New York World Telegram*, October 20, 1947.

7. *New York World Telegram*, October 23, 1947.

8. Isaac A. Hourwich, *Immigration and Labor* (New York: Putnam's Sons, 1912), p. 73.

9. Cited in Felix Cohen, *Immigration & National Welfare* (New York: League for Industrial Democracy), p. 21.

10. E. N. Saveth, *American Historians and European Immigrants* (New York: Columbia University Press, 1948), *passim.*

11. Hourwich, *op. cit.*, p. 63.

12. The illusion that immigration increases crime is an old one. The facts have been well studied; for example, President Hoover's National Commission on Law Observance and Enforcement dealt with the question in *Crime and the Foreign-Born* (Washington: 1931). The major conclusions have been summarized as follows in Donald Taft, *Human Migration* (New York: Ronald Press, 1936), p. 205; see also Donald Young, *American Minority Peoples* (New York: Harper & Brothers, 1932), Ch. VII.

1. The foreign-born commit fewer crimes per thousand of the same age and sex than do the native-born. For example, Chicago data showed the immigrant rate to be about a third of their "quota."

2. The foreign-born approach the crime record of the native-born most closely in crimes of violence, least closely in crimes for monetary gain.

3. The foreign-born commit fewer serious crimes per capita than do the natives, the rate being in general from one third to one half their quota.

4. The evidence does not permit one to say that any nationality is excessively criminal. The records of Japanese are especially good,

and those of orientals in general are good if one omits crimes associated with gambling.

   5. The evidence is insufficient to tell whether foreigners are prominent among professional gangsters or not.

   6. Neither are there sufficient data to enable one to judge as to the relative extent to which the children of foreigners are responsible for crime.

   Since juvenile delinquency occupies much public attention nowadays, it will be useful to examine the relation between it and the children of foreigners. Frederick M. Thrasher, as a result of his extensive investigations, concludes that "the children of immigrants do not form gangs more readily than the native-born of native stock living under similar conditions; the difference is primarily due to the fact that the latter live less frequently in gang-breeding areas." (Frederick M. Thrasher, "Are Our Criminals Foreigners?" *Our Racial and National Minorities*, p. 705.)

   The slum is the villain then—not the immigrant. Thrasher continues: "Further important evidence along the same line is the fact that the rates of delinquency for urban immigrant areas tend to remain unchanged and consistently high in spite of the fact that a succession of different immigrant groups occupies the same district over a long period of years. As a result of careful statistical studies in Chicago, Shaw states the illuminating conclusion that: 'The racial and nationality composition of the population in these areas of high rates of delinquents changed almost completely between 1900 and 1920, while the relative rates of delinquents remained practically unchanged.' Furthermore, the delinquency rates of the children and immigrant parents in delinquency areas show a decline when their parents move to better neighborhoods. Again Shaw concludes: 'As the older immigrant groups moved out of the areas of high rates of delinquents, the rates of delinquents among the children of these groups decreased and they tended to disappear from the juvenile court.'" Source: Clifford R. Shaw and Henry D. McKay, *Social Factors in Juvenile Delinquency*, p. 81 (Report on the Causes of Crime, Vol. II, Washington, National Commission on Law Observance and Enforcement).

   13. For a multitude of examples, see H. L. Mencken, *The American Language* (New York: Knopf, 1930-1948).

14. National Resources Committee, *The Problems of a Changing Population* (Washington: 1938), p. 127.

15. Robert E. Park, and Robert A. Miller, *Old World Traits Transplanted* (Chicago: Social Research Society, 1925).

16. *New York Evening Post*, Aug. 9, 1918, quoted by Park and Miller, *op. cit.*, p. 281.

17. E. George Payne, "Education and Cultural Pluralism," Brown and Roucek, eds. *Our Racial and National Minorities* (New York: Prentice-Hall, 1937), pp. 762-763.

18. George Saxon, "Immigrant Culture in a Stratified Economy," *Modern Review* (Feb. 1948), pp. 113-126.

19. National Committee on Immigration Policy, "Economic Aspects of Immigration" (New York: 1947), p. 18.

20. Claude McKay, *Harlem: The Negro Metropolis* (New York: Dutton, 1940), p. 90.

21. Between 1940 and 1945 the number of grocery stores in New York City dropped 22 per cent. Casualties numbered 3617. It is significant that "4/5ths of the stores that went out of business were in the poorest neighborhoods." Harlem showed a store death rate of 27.9 per cent. (New York Times, *Blue Prints for Sales*, 1945, pp. 5 and 18.) It may be argued that these figures reflect only war dislocations, but this does not explain away the situation. For one thing, only two of these five years (1942 and 1943) were marked by a net decrease in all businesses. For another, the same forces which operated during this period, i.e., greater pressure by the well-financed chains on the independents, led to a further concentration of economic power and profits.

22. National Committee on Immigration Policy, *Economic Aspects of Immigration* (New York: 1947), p. 23.

23. Cf. Note 3, Chapter II.

CHAPTER 6

1. U. S. Census, 1940, Puerto Rico, *Population*, Bulletin 3, p. 10.

2. Data on New York City from *New York City Market Analysis*. (New York: *New York Times* and other newspapers, 1943) p. IV; data on Puerto Rican rentals from U. S. Census, 1940, Puerto Rico, *Housing*, pp. 104–106.

3. U. S. Census, 1940, Puerto Rico, *Housing*, pp. 21, 24, 95, 97

4. Welfare Council, N.Y., *Puerto Ricans in N.Y.C.*, mimeographed edition.

5. U. S. Census, 1940, Puerto Rico, *Housing*, p. 27.

6. See Chapter III.

7. Robert E. Park, and H. A. Miller, *Old World Traits Transplanted* (New York, Harper & Brothers, 1921), p. 145.

8. *Ibid*, pp. 146, 242.

9. This population density is as of 1947. For figures on Puerto Rico, see Department of Agriculture and Commerce, *Annual Book of Statistics of Puerto Rico*, 1947, pp. 1–8; *Puerto Rican Monthly Statistical Report* (July–Sept., 1948), p. 29; for figure on New York, see Department of Commerce, *County Data Book* (Washington, 1947), p. 32.

10. Paquita Diaz, *Vocational Needs of Puerto Rican Migrants* (Rio Piedras: Social Science Research Center, 1947), p. 24.

11.

VOTE, BY RELIEF STATUS, SEX, AND TIME OF ARRIVAL

	Men				Women			
	Have been on relief		Never on relief		Have been on relief		Never on relief	
Ever voted?	Early	Recent	Early	Recent	Early	Recent	Early	Recent
Yes	80%	17%	80%	15%	65%	6%	50%	10%
No	20	83	20	85	35	94	50	90
TOTAL (100%)	(89)	(23)	(129)	(168)	(179)	(62)	(211)	(232)

12. The *media exposure* index was reduced in the following manner:

	Reads magazines		Does not read magazines	
	Reads newspapers once a week or more often	Reads newspapers less than once a week	Reads newspapers once a week or more often	Reads newspapers less than once a week
Attends movies once a week or more often				
Has a radio and listens	1*	2	2*	3
Has a radio but does not listen	1	2	2	3
Has no radio	2	3	3	3
Attends movies less than once a week				
Has a radio and listens	2	3	3*	3
Has a radio but does not listen	2	3	3	3
Has no radio	3	3	3	3

*More than a substantial majority of the migrants was classifiable in one of these three clusters.

CHAPTER 7

1. E. B. Reuter, *American Journal of Sociology*, 52, (September 2, 1946), p. 96.

2. Robert E. Park, and Herbert A. Miller, *Old World Traits Transplanted* (New York, Harper & Bros., 1921), p. 3.

3.

"Why Do You Think Americans Dislike Puerto Ricans?" by Sex and Race

	Men				Women			
	White	Int.	Negro	Total	White	Int.	Negro	Total
Refers to experiences reported by others	37%	64%	23%	40%	44%	49%	42%	44%
Reiterates New Yorkers' opinions[a]	26	17	36	25	23	20	23	22
Personal experience of discrimination	9	—	9	8	6	6	6	6
Refers to disliked qualities of New Yorkers	8	14	—	8	7	12	3	8
Refers to disliked qualities of Puerto Ricans	8	2	—	6	6	6	11	7
Others; don't know	12	3	32	13	14	7	15	13
TOTAL (100%)	(129)	(30)	(22)	(181)	(176)	(51)	(66)	(293)

[a] This category includes comments such as: "New Yorkers object to color and race"; "They think we are inferior"; comments to the effect that New Yorkers ascribe disliked qualities to Puerto Ricans; "They object to our language."

4.

"About How Many Americans in New York Believe That Puerto Ricans Are Inferior?" by Sex and Race

Number of Americans who think Puerto Ricans are inferior	Men				Women			
	White	Int.	Negro	Total	White	Int.	Negro	Total
All or many	34%	38%	26%	34%	28%	34%	29%	28%
Don't know	5	10	11	6	11	13	17	13
Some	49	44	47	48	48	49	40	46
None	12	8	16	12	13	4	14	13
TOTAL (100%)	(288)	(54)	(62)	(304)	(407)	(113)	(159)	(679)

5.

ATTITUDE TOWARDS WORKING WITH DIFFERENT ETHNIC GROUPS

	Men				Women			
	White	Int.	Negro	Total	White	Int.	Negro	Total
Americans								
like very much	43%	44%	51%	45%	40%	42%	36%	39%
doesn't matter	53	53	45	52	52	46	53	51
dislike	2	1	2	2	4	3	5	4
don't know	2	2	2	1	4	9	6	6
Puerto Ricans								
like very much	39%	53%	39%	41%	39%	45%	37%	39%
doesn't matter	55	40	48	51	46	42	46	46
dislike	5	5	11	6	10	5	11	10
don't know	1	2	2	2	5	8	6	5
Negroes								
like very much	17%	26%	29%	20%	8%	16%	16%	11%
doesn't matter	68	58	56	65	60	60	63	61
dislike	14	13	13	14	27	16	13	22
don't know	1	3	2	1	5	8	8	6
Italians								
like very much	24%	32%	34%	26%	17%	25%	27%	21%
doesn't matter	65	58	57	63	65	62	59	63
dislike	10	7	6	9	12	5	8	10
don't know	1	3	3	2	6	8	6	6
TOTAL (100%)	(293)	(57)	(65)	(415)	(418)	(117)	(160)	(695)

6.

ATTITUDE TO WORKING WITH ETHNIC GROUPS BY RACE, SEX, AND TIME OF ARRIVAL

	Men						Women					
	White		Int.		Negro		White		Int.		Negro	
	Rec.	Early	Rec.	Early	Rec.	Early	Rec.	Early	Rec.	Early	Rec.	Early
Americans												
like	41%	45%	49%	48%	50%	54%	40%	40%	49%	35%	42%	32%
doesn't matter	55	52	51	54	48	42	48	55	34	59	42	61
dislike	2	2	—	4	2	2	5	3	3	2	9	2
don't know	2	1	—	4	—	2	7	2	14	4	7	5
Puerto Ricans												
like	38%	40%	55%	50%	46%	29%	45%	35%	54%	35%	46%	30%
doesn't matter	56	54	42	38	41	59	38	52	33	53	40	51
dislike	4	6	3	8	13	8	10	10	3	7	8	14
don't know	2	—	—	4	—	4	7	3	10	5	6	5
Negroes												
like	20%	14%	33%	17%	29%	29%	7%	8%	12%	20%	18%	15%
doesn't matter	69	68	55	62	58	54	58	61	58	62	56	68
dislike	9	18	9	17	13	13	26	28	18	13	19	9
don't know	2	—	3	4	—	4	9	3	12	5	7	8
Italians												
like	24%	24%	33%	29%	31%	37%	17%	17%	27%	24%	32%	23%
doesn't matter	64	64	61	54	62	51	62	68	57	67	50	65
dislike	9	12	3	13	5	8	11	12	5	5	12	6
don't know	3	—	3	4	2	4	10	3	11	4	6	6
TOTAL (100%)	(124)	(169)	(33)	(24)	(40)	(25)	(166)	(242)	(61)	(56)	(62)	(98)

7.

HOW THE PUERTO RICANS COMPARE THEIR TREATMENT IN NEW YORK WITH
TREATMENT OF OTHER ETHNIC MINORITIES, BY SEX AND COLOR

	Men			Women		
	White	Int.	Negro	White	Int.	Negro
Latins						
better	8%	5%	10%	6%	7%	4%
same	70	72	72	64	57	64
worse	12	9	8	10	8	12
don't know	10	14	10	20	28	20
Italians						
better	14%	14%	10%	11%	6%	8%
same	48	39	62	45	48	45
worse	28	30	18	22	22	25
don't know	10	17	10	22	24	22
Jews						
better	2%	17%	7%	7%	7%	7%
same	65	34	54	42	37	45
worse	32	30	26	29	23	28
don't know	1	19	13	22	33	20
Negroes						
better	28%	17%	23%	21%	18%	22%
same	46	48	60	46	43	50
worse	18	19	11	15	16	12
don't know	8	16	6	18	23	16
TOTAL (100%)	(293)	(57)	(65)	(418)	(117)	(160)

CHAPTER 8

1. *Knowledge of English:* Each respondent rated himself on a
four-point scale according to whether he *understood* English "Well"
($+2$); "Moderately" ($+1$); "A little" (-1); or "Not at all" (-2).
The same system of rating was used for those who could *speak*
English "well," "moderately," "a little," or "not at all"; and for those
who could *read* the language "well," "moderately," "a little," or

"not at all." In this way a scale of Knowledge of English ranging from +6 to −6 was developed.

Speaks English	Understands English well				Understands English moderately			
	Reads well	Reads moderately	Reads a little	Reads not at all	Reads well	Reads moderately	Reads a little	Reads not at all
Well	6	5	3	2	5	4	2	1
Moderately	5	4	2	1	4	3	1	0
A little	3	2	0	−1	2	1	−1	−2
Not at all	2	1	−1	−2	1	0	−2	−3

Speaks English	Understands English a little				Understands English not at all			
Well	3	2	0	−1	2	1	−1	−2
Moderately	2	1	−1	−2	1	0	−2	−3
A little	0	−1	−3	−4	−1	−2	−4	−5
Not at all	−1	−2	−4	−5	−2	−3	−5	−6

2. *Public Use of English:* The respondents were asked whether they used English "frequently," "occasionally," or "never," in public situations such as at work, shopping, and in public places where there are Americans. They were scored +1 for each situation in which they used English frequently; 0 for each situation in which they used it occasionally, and −1 for each situation in which they never used it. In this way a scale of Public Use was developed ranging from +3 to −3.

Use English in public places where there are Americans	Use English at work frequently			Use English at work occasionally			Use English at work never		
	Use English while shopping			Use English while shopping			Use English while shopping		
	Frequently	Occasionally	Never	Frequently	Occasionally	Never	Frequently	Occasionally	Never
Frequently	3	2	1	2	1	0	1	0	−1
Occasionally	2	1	0	1	0	−1	0	−1	−2
Never	1	0	−1	0	−1	−2	−1	−2	−3

3. The *Language Proficiency* Index was arrived at by combining the respondent's scores on his Knowledge of English and on his

Public Use of English. The table was reduced in the following fashion:

Score on Public Use of English	Score on Knowledge of English				
	+4 to +6	3	2 to −2	−3	−4 to −6
+2 to +3	a	b	c	d	e
1	b	c	d	e	f
0	c	d	e	f	g
−1	d	e	f	g	h
−2 to −3	e	f	g	h	i

a–c = High language proficiency.
d–f = Intermediate.
g–i = Low language proficiency.

4. *Orientation Towards Official Agencies:* This index was established according to three variables. If the respondent was now on relief, he received a score of −1; if he was not on relief, he scored +1. If he answered the question, "What would you do if someone in this house needed money?" in terms of seeking institutionalized help, he scored −1; if he answered it in terms of seeking private help, he scored +1; if he didn't know how to answer the question, he was scored 0. And finally, his answer to the question, "What would you do if someone in your family had a personal problem that he could not solve?" was likewise scored −1 if he responded immediately in terms of seeking agency or institutional help; 0 if he didn't know; and +1 if his answer indicated that he would seek private or noninstitutional aid.

If needed money, would seek	Not now on relief			Now on relief		
	If needed help for family problems, would seek			If needed help for family problems, would seek		
	Personal help	Don't know	Agency help	Personal help	Don't know	Agency help
Personal help	3	2	1	1	0	−1
Don't know	2	1	0	0	−1	−2
Agency help	1	0	−1	−1	−2	−3

3 & 2 = Least oriented;   1 = Not oriented;   0 = Intermediate;   −1 = Oriented;
−2 & −3 = Most oriented.

5.

Language Proficiency, by Acknowledgment of Troubles

Language proficiency score	Have troubles	
	No	Yes
High	52%	40%
Intermediate	25	25
Low	23	35
Total (100%)	(585)	(430)

Orientation Towards Official Agencies, by Acknowledgment of Troubles

Agency orientation score	Have troubles	
	No	Yes
Not oriented	64%	49%
Intermediate	13	12
Oriented	23	39
Total (100%)	(585)	(430)

6. The *Adaptation Index* was reduced as follows:

Orientation Toward Official Agencies

Language proficiency	Least oriented		Not oriented		Intermediate		Oriented		Most oriented	
	Troubles		Troubles		Troubles		Troubles		Troubles	
	No	Yes	No	Yes	No	Yes	No	Yes	No	Yes
High	1	5	2	6	3	7	4	8	5	9
Intermediate	3	7	4	8	5	9	6	10	7	11
Low	5	9	6	10	7	11	8	12	9	13

1–4 = Most adapted.
5–9 = Intermediate.
10–13 = Least adapted.

7. The index of *Predisposition to Adapt* was reduced as follows:

	EDUCATION							
	High				Low			
	Male		Female		Male		Female	
	Under 35	35 and over	Under 35	35 and over	Under 35	35 and over	Under 35	35 and over
Employed								
White	1	3	3	5	3	5	5	7
Negro	2	4	4	6	4	6	6	8
Intermediate	3	5	5	7	5	7	7	9
Not Employed								
White	3	5	5	7	5	7	7	9
Negro	4	6	6	8	6	8	8	10
Intermediate	5	7	7	9	7	9	9	11

1–4 = High predisposition.
5–7 = Intermediate predisposition.
8–11 = Low predisposition.

*Appendix I: The Questions**

Do you speak Spanish? ____Yes, ____no. Were you born in Puerto Rico? ____Yes, ____no. (*If respondent was not born in Puerto Rico, do not interview*).

1. When did you arrive in New York (the last trip)? Month? Year?
2A. Have you ever been to N.Y. before? ____Yes, ____no.
2B. (If "Yes" to 2A, ask:) Not counting the present trip, how many times have you been in N.Y. before? (*Fill in for each trip:*) What year(s)? How long did you stay? Were you visiting, planning to stay, on business, or something else? Why did you leave?
3. Have you ever lived anywhere outside Puerto Rico other than N.Y.? ____Yes, ____no. (*If "Yes" to 3, fill in for each residence:*) Where? What year(s)? How long did you stay? Why did you go there? What things about your life in these other places made you want to leave them?
4. Where in P.R. did you live just before you left (the last time)? How about before that? (*Fill in for each of last 3 residences in P.R.—omit residences outside of P.R.:*) Name of Municipio? Was it city or country? What year(s)? How long did you live there?
5. Where in P.R. were you born? Was it city or country?
6. About how long before you left P.R. (the last time) did you seriously have in mind the idea of leaving? ____less than a month, ____from a month to a year, ____more than a year.
7. When you came to N.Y. (the last time) did you intend to visit

---

* This is a translation from the Spanish guide. In this draft we have changed the format of the questionnaire in order to compress it. The guide-as-used was of course openly spaced to permit detailed answers. The italicized remarks in parenthesis are instructions to the interviewers. In addition to personal field instructions and supervision, a set of printed instructions concerning the use of the questionnaire was given to each interviewer.

or to settle down permanently, or something else? (*If "Something else," ask:*) What?

8. (a) Would you tell me in your own words why you left P.R. and came to N.Y.?

(b) Can you think of anything else?

9. (a) What things about the life in P.R. made you want to leave P.R.?

(b) What things about the life in N.Y. interested you in coming to N.Y.?

10. Was it more (*Insert things about P.R.*) or more (*Insert things about N.Y.*) that made you want to make the change? ____N.Y., ____P.R., ____both equally.

11. How did you learn (*Insert things mentioned in 9b*) about N.Y.?

12. While you were still living in P.R.:

(a) Did you *hear* anyone in particular say anything about N.Y.? ____Yes, ____no. (*If "Yes," ask:*) Who (relationship)? Had they ever been to N.Y.? What did they say?

(b) Did you happen to *ask* anyone in particular about N.Y.? ____Yes, ____no. (*If "Yes," ask:*) Who (relationship)? Had they ever been to N.Y.? What did they say?

(c) Did you get any letters about N.Y. from any people already living here? ____Yes, ____no. (*If "Yes," ask:*) Who (relationship)? What did they say?

(d) Did you read anything about N.Y. in the newspapers? ____Yes, ____no. (*If "Yes," ask:*) What? Was it an advertisement, or not?

Remember, this is while you were still in P.R.:

(e) Did you learn anything about N.Y. in magazines? ____Yes, ____no. (*If "Yes," ask:*) What?

(f) Did you see anything about N.Y. in the movies? ____Yes, ____no. (*If "Yes," ask:*) What?

(g) Did you hear anything about N.Y. on the radio? ____Yes, ____no. (*If "Yes," ask:*) What did you hear?

(h) Did you get to know anything about N.Y. in any other way before you came? ____Yes, ____no. (*If "Yes," ask:*) In what way?

13. Which of all these do you think gave you the most information about N.Y.? (*Read:*) magazines, letters from N.Y., people you

heard, radio, people you asked, movies or newspapers? Other? (*Specify*).

14. Who had the idea of your leaving P.R. and coming to N.Y.— you or somebody else? (*If "Somebody else," ask:*) Who (relationship)?

15. When you came to N.Y. (the last time) did you (*Read:*) come alone, with other members of your family: whom (relationship)?, with friends, or in a group organized by some agency: what agency?

16. Did anyone or any agency lend or give you money or a ticket to help you come to N.Y.? ____Yes, ____no. (*If "Yes," ask:*) Was it a ticket or money? (*If money:*) How much? Who (relationship) or what (agency)? Were they (or was it) in P.R. or in N.Y. at the time?

17. (a) While you were living in P.R. about to come to N.Y. what were you doing? ____working for pay, ____self-employed, ____housewife, ____unpaid family worker, ____not employed. (*"If Not employed," ask:*) Were you looking for work or not (*If "Not looking," ask:*) Was that because: ____you were too young, ____student in school, ____ill, ____retired or pensioned, ____on relief, or ____something else? (*If "Something else," specify:*)

   (b) While you were still living in P.R. about to come to N.Y., what did you expect to do in N.Y.? (*Read:*) Try to get any job you could, try to get a particular kind of job you had in mind, open your own business, be a housewife, or something else? (*If "Something else," specify:*)

   (c) In case you weren't able to earn or get a living, did you think you might get some kind of aid? ____Yes, ____no. (*If "Yes," ask:*) From where?

18. If, for some reason, it had been impossible for you to come to N.Y., what would you have done. (*Read:*) Stayed in P.R., or gone somewhere else? (*If "Somewhere else," ask:*) Where? Why there?

19. Back on the island, when you were thinking about leaving P.R., did you ever consider going to live some place other than N.Y.? (*If "Yes," ask:*) Where? How did you happen to consider (*Insert place mentioned*)? Why did you give up the idea?

20. Now that you are here, do you intend to visit or to settle permanently, or something else? (*If "Something else," ask:*) What?

(*If respondent does not plan to stay in N.Y. permanently, or isn't sure, ask 21, 22, 23*)

21. Where do (or would) you plan to go? _____Back to P.R.? (*If "Yes," ask:*) What do you plan to do when you get there? Why that? _____Somewhere else? (*If "Yes," ask:*) Where? What do you plan to do when you get there? _____Just any place or don't know? (*If "Yes," ask:*) What do you mean?

22. When do you plan to go there?

23. Would you tell me in your own words why you plan to leave N.Y. and go to (*Insert place named*)?

(*If respondent does plan to stay in N.Y., ask 24*)

24. Have you ever thought of leaving N.Y. and going somewhere else? _____Yes, _____no. (*If "Yes," ask:*) Where? What made you think of going there? Why do you think you haven't gone there?

25. While you were still living in P.R., did you think that in N.Y.:
    (a) You would have to do *harder* work or *not so hard* work as in P.R.?
    (b) Did you think you would have *more* personal independence or *less* personal independence than in P.R.?
    (c) Remember, this is before you left P.R.: Did you think that you would have *more* free time for yourself in N.Y. or *less* free time for yourself?
    (d) Did you think that you would feel *more* "rushed" in N.Y. than in P.R. or *less* rushed?
    (*Indicate for each of the above, one of the following:*)
    _____More, _____about the same, _____less, _____never thought about it.

26. Who is the head of this household? (*Fill in for each household member:*) Relation to head (*Identify respondent*)? Sex? Age? Year arrived in N.Y.? Employment and occupation?* Weekly earnings? Household contribution: Money or duties? Going to remain or visiting?

27. In P.R., before you came here, what kind of arrangement did you have about the house or apartment you lived in?

* See Question 17 (a) for check-list on this question.

_____Owner occupied, or _____rented, _____squatters, not paying rent, _____owned by relatives, paying little or no rent, _____tenant cottage, _____other (*Specify*).

28. What was your usual job in P.R. just before you came to N.Y.? Did you work for some company or individual, some family member, or for yourself? How much did you make a week? How long did you have this job? (*Get last 3 jobs in P.R., fill in the above for each job. If unemployed or on relief indicate periods, get a continuous record.*)

29. During the last 2 years you were in P.R. about how many months out of each year did you work?

30. Have you ever had a job of any kind in N.Y.? _____Yes, _____no. (*Ask of all who answer "Yes:"*) What is your present occupation? Do you work for some company or individual, some family member, or for yourself? How much do you make a week? How long have you had this job? (*Get last 3 jobs in P.R. and first job in N.Y. Fill in above for each job. If unemployed or on relief indicate periods.*)

(*Ask Questions 31 and 32 only of those who answer "Yes" to Question 30.*)

31. How did you get your *first* job here in N.Y. (the last time you came to N.Y.)? Did you have it before you came or did you get it after you were here? (*If "Had it before," ask:*) How did that happen? _____Came on contract from P.R.: agency? or _____someone already here arranged it for me: Who (relationship)?

(*If "Got it after here," ask:*) How did that happen? _____ Through an agency: What agency?, or _____Friend told me about it: Who (relationship)?

32. How did you get the job you *now* have? (*Or job last held if now unemployed*) _____Through an agency: What? _____Friend (family) told me about it, or took me: Who (relationship)?, _____Self-employed, or _____other (Specify).

33. Have you ever sent any money or ticket to someone to come to N.Y.? _____Yes, _____no. (*If "Yes," ask:*) Who (relationship)? How much?

34. (a) Do you more or less regularly send money to anyone in P.R.? _____Yes, _____no. (*If "Yes," ask:*) Who (relationship)? How often? Usually how much do you send?

(b) Do you more or less regularly receive money from anyone living in P.R.? ____Yes, ____no. (If "Yes," ask:) Who (relationship)? How often? How much do you usually receive?

35. (a) What do you personally most want out of your own life? *Why* is that? Anything else?

(b) Are you the sort of person who thinks very much, just sometimes, or not so much about how you might get that?

(c) Are you doing anything that you feel might help you get that out of life? ____Yes, ____no. (If "Yes," ask:) What? (If "No," ask:) Why not?

36. In general, how do you feel about your present job—Do you like it or not?

37. (a) What kind of an occupation would you most like to have?

(b) What do you think your chances are of getting it in the next 3 or 4 years? ____excellent, ____good, ____average, ____little, ____none, or ____don't know.

(c) Are you doing anything which will help you get that kind of work? ____Yes, ____no. (If "Yes," ask:) What are you doing? (If "No," ask:) Why not?

38. Which would you prefer, to work little and earn enough to live on, or to work more and earn more than enough to live on?

39. Which of these statements best agrees with your way of thinking? ____I spent too much time in school, ____I spent enough time in school, ____I would like to have spent a little more time in school, or ____I should have liked to spend much more time in school.

(Ask Questions 40, 41, 42 and 43 of all—whether they have children or not)

40. What occupation would you like your children (If *you had any*) to follow?

41. Regardless of what you hope, what do you think it's most likely that he (or she) will do? Why do you say that?

42. How many years of school would you like your children to have?

43. How many years of school do you think your children will have if your situation remains as it is?

44. On the whole do you like to live in N.Y. or not?

45. (a) Could you tell what you *like best* about living in N.Y.?
    (b) What else do you like here?
46. (a) What do you *like least* about living in N.Y.?
    (b) What else don't you like about it?
47. (a) In your opinion, do Americans generally like or generally dislike the Puerto Ricans here in N.Y.?
    (b) Why do you think so?
48. Do Americans treat Puerto Ricans better or worse than they do (*Ask concerning each of the following:*) Negroes? Italians? Jews? Other Latins? _____Better, _____same, _____worse. (*If "worse," ask in each case:*) Why?
49. In general, how do you feel about working in the same place with (*Ask concerning each of the following:*) Americans? Puerto Ricans? Latins? Negroes? Italians? _____Like it very well, _____doesn't matter, _____don't like it.
50. About how many Americans in N.Y. believe that Puerto Ricans are inferior? _____All of them, _____many of them, _____some of them, _____none.
51. (a) What is your religion? _____Roman Catholic, _____Protestant, _____Sect (pentecostal, etc.), _____Spiritualist (only), _____No religion.
    (b) (*If respondent doesn't answer "Spiritualist" above, ask:*) Do you believe in Spiritualism?
52. Which of the following statements best describes your personal attitude towards religion? (*Read:*) _____Religion is the most important thing in my life, _____Religion is important in my life, _____I am religious in my own way, _____I oppose religion.
53. Do you go to religious services in N.Y.? _____Yes, _____no. (*If "Yes," ask:*) About how often do you go?
54. Did you go more frequently to religious services in P.R. or do you go more often to religious services here in N.Y.? _____More in P.R., _____more in N.Y., _____the same. How does this happen?
55. About how often do you use English (*Fill in whether "Frequently," "Occasionally," or "Never" in each of the following:*) For conversation with other adults of this household? Talking with children in the household? On the job? Buying things in stores? Chatting with friends? In public places where there are Americans, such as subways, buses?

56. How about your way of living in N.Y.?
    (a) Is your work harder or not so hard as it was in P.R.?
    (b) Do you have *more* personal independence or *less* personal independence than in P.R.?
    (c) Do you have *more* free time for yourself in N.Y. or *less* free time for yourself than you did in P.R.?
    (d) Do you feel *more* "rushed" to do things in N.Y. than in P.R. or *less* rushed?
    (*Indicate for each of the above:*)____More (harder), ____ about the same, ____Less (not so hard), ____never thought about it.

57. Could you tell me what associations, organizations, clubs, regular meeting groups you belong to? (*Get for each one:*) What are their names? What type of activity do they perform? About how often do you get together?

58. Do you or does any member of this household belong to a union? ____Yes, ____no. (*If "Yes," ask:*) Who (Specify)? Which union do you (and/or they) belong to? How often do you (and/or they) go to meetings? (*If "No," ask:*) Have you ever belonged to a union? (*If "Have ever belonged," ask:*) Where—was it in P.R. or N.Y.? (*If "N.Y." ask:*) Why don't you belong now?

59. Have you any real friends here in N.Y.? ____Yes, ____no. (*If "Yes," ask:*) About how many: a whole lot, a few, only one, or none? (*If "No," ask:*) Why not?

60. Is it harder or easier to get together with friends here in N.Y. than in P.R. (and why)? ____Harder in N.Y., ____same, ____easier in N.Y.

61. Whereabouts are you *most* likely to get together with your friends? ____In each other's apartments, ____eating or drinking places, ____at formal club meetings, ____on the street corner, ____at grocery stores or market, ____dance halls or cabarets, ____on the job, or ____other (*Specify*).

62. Where is it harder to get to have real friends: in N.Y. or in P.R. (and why)? ____Harder in N.Y., ____same, ____harder in P.R.

63. What newspaper, or newspapers, do you read? How often do you read them?

64. (a) Is there a radio in the apartment? ____Yes, ____no. (If "Yes," ask:)

   (b) Are you *more* apt to listen to Spanish or to American programs?

   (c) When do you usually listen to the radio?

65. (a) About how often do you go to the movies?

   (b) What kind of films do you prefer to see, Latin *or* American?

66. Are there any magazines which you read more or less regularly? ____Yes, ____no. (If "Yes") Which ones?

67. (a) About how well do you understand the English language?

   (b) Do you read it?

   (c) Do you speak it?

   (d) Do you write it?

   (*Indicate for each:*) ____Well, ____moderately, ____little, ____none.

68. Everybody occasionally has troubles: Has anything in particular been troubling you lately? ____Yes, ____no. (If "Yes," ask:) What? Are you doing anything about it? ____Yes, ____no. (If "Yes,") What?

69. (a) What would you do if you were unemployed and couldn't find a job?

   (b) (If *agency not named, ask:*) Do you know of any *place* which is set up to help people find jobs? ____Yes, ____no. (*If agency named in 69(a) or "Yes" in 69(b):*) Where is it? How did you learn about it?

70. Have you or anyone in this household ever gone to such a place? ____Yes, ____no. (If "Yes":) Who (relationship)? What place, and where is it? Did they get you (them) a job or not?

71. (a) What would you do if you or some member of this household needed money to help pay for such things as rent, food, or clothes?

   (b) (If *agency not named, ask:*) Do you know of any *place* to go for such help? ____Yes, ____no. (*If agency named in 71(a) or "Yes" in 71(b), ask:*) Where is it? How did you learn about it?

72. Have you ever heard of N.Y. relief? ____Yes, ____no. (If "Yes," ask:) Did you learn about it while you were still in P.R.

or after you got to N.Y.? How long does someone have to be in N.Y. before he can get on relief?

73. Have you ever been on relief? _____Yes, _____no. (If "Yes," ask:) Were you on relief in N.Y. or in P.R. or in both places? (If "In New York," ask:)

    (a) How long were you (have you been) on relief in N.Y.? What years?

    (b) Beside giving you money, did they do anything for you? _____Yes, _____no. (If "Yes," ask:) What?

    (c) Did you, on the whole, like your case worker, or not? (If "No," ask:) Why not?

74. Can you tell me what Social Security is—I mean what does it do?

75. (a) Do you have a Social Security card?

    (b) Are you getting any money from Social Security? _____Yes, _____no. (If "Yes," ask:) How much?

76. (a) What would you do if you or somebody in this household had an illness that couldn't be taken care of at home?

    (b) (If no agency named, ask:) Do you know of any place you can call or go to for help in such a case? _____Yes, _____no. (If agency named in 76(a) or "Yes" in 76(b), ask:) Where is it? How did you learn about it?

77. Have you been sick any time during the last year? _____Yes, _____no. (If "Yes," ask:) What was done to cure your illness? What was the matter? Did you go to bed? _____Yes, _____no. (If "Yes":) For how long?

78. Have you ever heard of anyone in N.Y. who cures with "spiritual remedies"? _____Yes, _____no. (If "Yes," ask:) Have you or a member of your household ever consulted anyone in N.Y. who cures with "spiritual remedies"?

79. (a) What would you do if someone in your family had lung trouble (tuberculosis)?

    (b) Has anyone in your family ever had lung trouble? _____Yes, _____no. (If "Yes," ask:) Who (specify)? Was anything done about it? (If "Yes":) What? (Then ask:) Have you ever had lung trouble?

80. (a) Where would you go for a blood examination (V.D., syphilis)?

(b) Has anyone in your family ever had blood trouble? ____Yes, ____no. (If "Yes," ask:) Who (specify)? Was anything done about it? (If "Yes":) What? (Then ask:) Have *you* ever had blood trouble?

81. (a) What would you do if you (your wife or daughter) became pregnant and needed care?

(b) (If *no agency named, ask:*) Do you know of any agency where one can get help for this? ____Yes, ____no. (If *agency named in 81(a) or if "Yes" to 81(b), ask:*) Where is it? How did you learn about it?

82. Have you (your wife or daughter) ever needed this type of care? ____Yes, ____no. (If "Yes," ask:) Who (relationship)? What was done about it?

(Ask Questions 83, 84, 85, 86, and 87 only where there are children under 18.)

83. Do you know if there is any place near here where people can leave their children during the day? ____Yes, ____no. (If "Yes," ask:) Where is it? How did you learn about it? Do any children of this household go there?

84. Do any children living in this household ever go to any play center or playground or not? ____Yes, ____no. (If "Yes," ask:) Do they go alone, with you, or with some other adult?

85. Are any of the children under six in this household ever seen by a doctor or a nurse when they are *not* sick? ____Yes, ____no. (If "Yes," ask:) Where? How did you learn about it? How often do they (he, she) see the doctor or nurse there?

86. Do your children eat the lunch served at school? ____Yes, ____no. (If "Yes," ask:) How many times a week? (If "No," ask:) Do they take their lunches with them from home, buy it, or what?

87. Do any children living in this household take cod liver oil? ____Yes, ____no. (If "Yes," ask:) How often?

88. (a) What would you do if you had some problem in your family you couldn't solve? (I mean problems like trouble with your husband (wife), misbehaving children, caring for old people, or things like that?)

(b) (If *no agency named*) Do you know of any place to go for help with such problems? ____Yes, ____no. (If *agency named in 88(a) or if "Yes" in 88(b), ask:*) Where is it? How did you learn about it?

89. Have you ever been to such an agency? ____Yes, ____no. (If "Yes," ask:) Did they help you or not? (If "No," ask:) Have any of your friends or anyone you know of gone to such a place? (If someone "has gone," ask:) Who (relationship)? Did they feel they were helped or not?

90. Where do you go for recreation in your free time? . . . Any other place? (For each place mentioned ask:) How often do you go? Do you go with someone? (If "Yes":) With whom (relationship)?

91. If you could choose, what two things would you most like to do for recreation in your free time?

92. Since you have been living in New York have you ever called a policeman for help or for any other reason? ____Yes, ____no. (If "Yes," ask:) For what?

93. Since living in New York have you ever gone to court for anything? ____Yes, ____no. (If "Yes," ask:) What for? Did anyone help you arrange this? ____Yes, ____no. (If someone "helped," ask:) Who or what?

94. (Observe physical type:) ____white, ____indio, ____grifo, ____mulatto, ____Negro.

95. (a) What was the last grade you completed in school? Read? Write?

    (b) Did you ever go to any trade or business or vocational or night school? ____Yes, ____no. (If "Yes":) What school? Was it in P.R. or in N.Y.? How long did you go there?

96. What is your present marital status? ____single, ____legal marriage, ____living together (consensual marriage), ____legal marriage, broken by desertion, separation, annulment, or divorce, ____consensual marriage, broken by desertion or separation, ____legal marriage terminated by death, ____consensual marriage broken by death, ____concubine (one of the parties is married to someone else).

97. Are you a veteran, or the wife, or the parent of a veteran?

98. Have you ever voted in an election in New York City?

99. (a) What was your father doing about the time you left school? (Usual occupation)

    (b) What did your mother do about the time you left school? ____Not working, ____a housewife, ____working: at what?

100. Is there a refrigerator or icebox in the apartment?
101. How many rooms are there in the apartment (*Not counting kitchen and bathroom*)?

Name of respondent:_____ Others present during interview:
Address: Apt. No._____ Floor_____
        Street & Number_____
        Borough_____ Sample Unit_____ Name of interviewer:
Date of interview_____
Time began:_____ Time ended:_____

Skin	Hair	Lips	Nose
____white	____kinky	____thick	____narrow–thin
____tan	____wavy	____medium	____medium
____brown	____straight	____thin	____broad–fleshy
____black			

Appendix II: The Sample

The Puerto Ricans in this survey do not represent a cross section of *all* Puerto Ricans in New York City; they represent a cross section of all *adult* Puerto Ricans born in Puerto Rico and now residing in the two *core areas*, the places of most concentration, of New York City.

To obtain a sample of all Puerto Ricans in New York, adult or otherwise, was impossible due to the lack of adequate information concerning the Puerto Ricans in the city, and the obvious limitations of our budget for this study.

The usual method of cross-section sampling by the quota method could not be used because of the absence of over-all information concerning the Puerto Ricans with which to control our sample. There were even no reliable estimates of the number of Puerto Ricans living in the city. Such limited characteristics of this population as revealed by the 1940 census were not sufficient to indicate the composition of the population because of the swiftly changing conditions of the population since the war—as revealed by immigration records—and also because of the absence in even this outdated source of any economic information, one of the most important controls necessary for this type of quota sampling.

Another way to obtain a cross section of all Puerto Ricans in New York City would have been to take a complete census enumeration of the entire city ourselves, covering the items necessary for the establishment of quota control. Then on the basis of this information, a quota sample of all Puerto Ricans in New York could be interviewed in detail on the subject of our study. Such a procedure was obviously beyond the financial limits of our survey.

The alternative left us, therefore, was to conduct an area sample. But again, this could not be done for the entire city. Any area sample of all the Puerto Ricans in New York City would require the classification of all blocks in the city known to contain any Puerto Ricans according to their relative density. We would then have blocks that were less than 10 per cent Puerto Rican, 10–24 per cent, 25–49 per cent, 50–74 per cent, 75–89 per cent, and 90 per cent or more. A sample of the blocks in each area would then be picked at random; but since our information lead us to believe that three-quarters of all Puerto Rican blocks would fall into the 10 per cent and 25 per cent groups, we would have had to sample large numbers of blocks which contain only a few Puerto Ricans—an enumeration of from 50 to 100 households in order to reach one Puerto Rican household. This, again, plus the fact that it would be another major job to locate all these scattered areas of less dense Puerto Rican population, made the sampling of all the Puerto Ricans in New York unfeasible.

We therefore decided to conduct an area sample in the areas of largest concentration. Each borough of New York was inspected by means of all available ecological material in order to locate "the core areas."

A. Location of Core Areas

The general location of the Puerto Ricans in New York City with respect to the five boroughs can be quickly spotted with reference to the censuses of 1930 and 1940, in which around three-quarters of them are seen to reside in Manhattan.

PUERTO RICAN-BORN PERSONS IN NEW YORK CITY

	1930	1940
Bronx	3%	13%
Brooklyn	18	15
Manhattan	77	70
Queens	2	2
Richmond	—	—
TOTAL	100%	100%

Marked changes in the distribution of the Puerto Ricans occurred between 1930 and 1940, and have most likely occurred since 1940 due to the increased postwar migration to the city, but this information enabled us at least confidently to restrict our investigation of the core areas to three of the five boroughs: Bronx, Brooklyn, and Manhattan.

Within each of these boroughs we had the help of various agencies in segregating the blocks according to approximate density of Puerto Ricans. A city department, the nature of whose work compels us to refer to it as Agency X, gave us verbal information on the concentration of Puerto Ricans, block by block in each of the boroughs. A report prepared by a committee of the Association of Assistant Superintendents, "A Program of Education for Puerto Ricans in New York City" (1947), gave us the number of Puerto Rican-born students and the students with Puerto Rican parents by each of the 51 supervisory (geographical) areas in the city. Further information was supplied from a report by the Pathfinding Service under the directorship of David Barry, "The Protestant Church and Puerto Ricans in New York City," which located 63 Protestant Spanish-speaking churches in the city, all of which were led by native Puerto Rican ministers. The addresses of these churches were made available to us, and again indicated the clusters of Puerto Ricans. Finally, an importing firm was kind enough to provide us with the addresses of some 800 Spanish retail grocery stores, and some cigar and stationery stores. Although these stores were not exclusively Puerto Rican, the interest of the importer was, so they gave fairly reliable indices of Puerto Rican communities large enough to warrant special stores.

MANHATTAN: In Manhattan, the borough which contains the largest number of Puerto Ricans, they live in eleven locality groups. The main one is, of course, "Spanish" Harlem—between 100th and 125th Street, east of Fifth Avenue to Third Avenue. There 59 per cent of all the Puerto Rican school children in Manhattan live, comprising 30 per cent of the total school enrollment in that district. Forty-three per cent of the grocery stores and 75 per cent of the Protestant Puerto Rican churches are in this big neighborhood. Agency X estimated that 100,000 Puerto Ricans lived in this area, most of the blocks rating from 50 to 75 per cent Puerto Ricans.

Three smaller but distinct groups emerge. LaSalle Street, Moylan Place, and 125th Street west of Amsterdam to 150th Street form the next densest section. There 18 per cent of the school enrollment is Puerto Rican, 19 per cent of the grocery stores serve this area, and there is one church. Agency X estimates 42,000 in this area. Central Park West between 106th Street and Cathedral Parkway is a small but concentrated section where 16 per cent of the school enrollment

is Puerto Rican; 12 per cent of the Puerto Rican grocery stores are
in this section. And then in a small area of Chelsea north of 14th
Street around 8th and 9th Avenues, 15 per cent of the school enrollment is Puerto Rican.

ECOLOGICAL AREAS OF MANHATTAN

District	Puerto Rican School Children	Spanish Grocery Stores	Puerto Rican Protestant Churches
East Side			
1. Lower East Side	731	5	2
2. Second Avenue	808	3	1
3. Marginal Harlem	307	1	—
4. Spanish Harlem	7091	88	24
5. Lenox Avenue	243	8	—
West Side			
6. Greenwich Village	178	2	—
7. Chelsea	294	10	—
8. Amsterdam, San Juan Hill	750	10	—
9. Central Park West	394	25	2
10. Lasalle	1108	39	1
11. Washington Heights	725	16	2

The remaining localities are: (1) the lower East Side, where
Puerto Ricans are scattered east of the Bowery from the Williamsburgh Bridge to 14th Street; (2) on both sides of Second Avenue
from 14th to 58th Streets; (3) on the southern fringes of Harlem
from 86th to 96th Streets; (4) along Lenox Avenue north of Central
Park to 140th Street. The last is sparsely settled—a marginal area
north of Spanish Harlem similar to the one south of it.

Less important are the small groups in the Greenwich Village area
around Hudson and Grove Streets; on either side of Amsterdam
Avenue from 52nd Street north to 86th Street covering the old San
Juan Hill area; and in Washington Heights between 160th and
180th Streets.

The Puerto Rican areas are characteristically low-income neighborhoods, with the Lasalle, Amsterdam, and Washington Heights neighborhoods being slightly above the others ($35 monthly rentals com-
pared with the $25 average of the other).

THE BRONX: In the Bronx, the area most densely populated with Puerto Ricans (less than 50 per cent) spreads out over a large part of the district known as Morrisania, around the intersection of Westchester and Prospect Avenues. A newer settlement than Spanish Harlem, Morrisania also differs in appearance. Spanish Harlem usually contains buildings of ten or more dwelling units; Morrisania has few such large units and is mostly composed of one- and two-family houses, and thus the Puerto Ricans are spread over a larger area. Agency X estimated 72,000 Puerto Ricans in Morrisania; 77 per cent (148) of the Spanish stores in the Bronx, ten churches, and 50 per cent of the Puerto Rican children in Bronx public schools are located in this region.

ECOLOGICAL AREAS OF THE BRONX

District	Puerto Rican School Children	Spanish Grocery Stores	Puerto Rican Protestant Churches
1. Morrisania	3826	148	10
2. Crotona Park—South	1032	17	—
3. Crotona Park—West	512	6	—
4. Mott Haven	1620	15	—
5. Highbridge	275	3	—

Two fringe settlements spread out from the major core area. Just to the north of Morrisania, up to Crotona Park, reside 13 per cent of the Bronx Puerto Rican school children who form 9 per cent of the district school enrollment, and there are 17 Spanish grocery stores. Continuing from here on west around the park there is another small nucleus around Claremont Parkway.

Larger than these two fringes but smaller than Morrisania is the area centered in Mott Haven at the southernmost tip of the Bronx, roughly St. Anne's Avenue and 138th Street. Twenty-one per cent of the Bronx Puerto Rican children reside here, representing 9 per cent of the school enrollment for the district, which is rather compact and includes 15 of the stores.

Lastly, in the Highbridge area west of Mott Haven and east of the Harlem River, there are three widely separated stores and 3 per cent of the school children. This is the only other specific area with sufficient numbers of Puerto Ricans to be considered separately.

These five groups account for 95 per cent of the public schools with Puerto Rican children, all the churches, and all but four of the 193 stores in the Bronx. The remaining school children are loosely clustered throughout the borough from New York University to Riverdale on the west side and from Throgg's Neck to Woodlawn Cemetery in the eastern section, areas considerably higher socioeconomically than those containing the main clusters of Puerto Ricans.

BROOKLYN: The Puerto Ricans in Brooklyn reside in several thinly populated groups. The only well-defined cluster is the Stuyvesant area around the intersection of Flushing Avenue and Broadway: here are 36 per cent of all the Puerto Rican school children in Brooklyn and 34 retail grocery stores. This is principally a residential district of one- and two-family houses.

In the Brooklyn Navy Yard area, the original settlement of Puerto Ricans in New York City, are 13 per cent of the Puerto Rican children in Brooklyn schools, and 11 stores. In South Brooklyn, below the fashionable Brooklyn Heights area, there is another cluster spread out along Columbia Avenue; primarily an industrial area, it houses the families of stevedores who work around the docks. Continuing south, to the west of Greenwood Cemetery and along Third Avenue is another district, largely residential and accounting for 4 per cent of the Puerto Rican school children in Brooklyn.

Lastly, there are two other clusters: one at the foot of the Williamsburgh Bridge, a dense tenement house section; and in Greenpoint, an industrial area with poor housing facilities.

ECOLOGICAL AREAS OF BROOKLYN

District	Puerto Rican School Children	Spanish Grocery Stores
1. Brooklyn Navy Yard	618	11
2. South Brooklyn	718	15
3. Greenwood Cemetery	171	3
4. Stuyvesant	1686	34
5. Williamsburgh	480	8
6. Greenpoint	25	1

This accounts for 79 per cent of the Puerto Rican school children in Brooklyn and all of the stores; the remaining Puerto Ricans are spread over the rest of the borough.

With the core areas of Puerto Rican settlement in New York thus roughly established, we then decided to study the three largest core areas: Spanish Harlem, Morrisania, and the Stuyvesant area of Brooklyn. Preliminary calculations of the number of Puerto Ricans in these areas called for 700 interviews in Spanish Harlem, 500 in Morrisania, and 100 in Stuyvesant.

B. *The Area Sample*

It was originally decided to select at random half the blocks in each of the core areas for study. Each interviewer was assigned to a specific corner of a specific block. He was to enumerate the block, going around it clockwise and recording on his route sheet the address of each building and the number of apartments in it.

Starting with the first building on the assigned corner, he counted the apartments clockwise, from left to right, on each floor within the building until he came to the tenth apartment. There he determined if there were any Puerto Rican adults over eighteen years of age in the household. If it was a Puerto Rican household, he made an interview; if not, he indicated that fact on his route sheet, and continued counting to the next tenth apartment.

The household member to be interviewed was selected with the aid of a table of random numbers since we did not have data on the composition of the Puerto Rican population or households as a basis for determining a cross-section sample. (Also, as in every instance of a house-to-house survey, to interview just anyone who is home provides a bias toward housewives and an underenumeration of the working population.) If the household member who should be interviewed according to the random number sheet was not at home, an appointment was made to meet with him at another time.

Soon after our field work started it became apparent that the estimates of the number of Puerto Ricans in these core areas, upon which our survey factor was based, were overstated. Since there turned out to be fewer Puerto Ricans living in the blocks, to take every tenth dwelling unit in one half the blocks would not result in enough interviews for analysis. Therefore, two changes were made in our method of sampling.

First, in both Spanish Harlem and Morrisania, still taking every tenth dwelling unit, we increased the sample blocks to include the entire core areas: in Spanish Harlem this consisted of 66 blocks; in the less densely populated area of Morrisania, 80 blocks, in which 20,000 dwelling units were contacted in order to reach 500 Puerto Ricans.

Second, in Brooklyn the overestimation of the number of Puerto Ricans turned out to be very great. As the number of Puerto Ricans in the core area was much less and more scattered than even in Morrisania, to obtain 100 interviews would have meant interviewing every third, fourth, or fifth household in many scattered blocks at a cost prohibitive to our budget. In short, it turned out that there were no core areas in Brooklyn of the sort in Manhattan and the Bronx. We therefore decided to eliminate Brooklyn from our survey.

We obtained interviews which averaged about an hour and a quarter in 81 per cent of the Bronx Puerto Rican households and 85 per cent of the Manhattan households. There was an over-all mortality of 12 per cent: among 7 per cent neither the selected respondent nor any other member was home after three or four visits; at only 5 per cent of the households were our interviewers refused admittance, despite recent unfavorable newspaper publicity concerning the Puerto Ricans, which might have increased refusal to be interviewed.

In this way, by first spotting the core areas on the basis of all ecological data and our own informal field work, we located the two most important core areas of Puerto Rican settlement—Spanish Harlem in Manhattan and Morrisania in the Bronx. And by a systematic coverage of every tenth household in the 66 blocks in Spanish Harlem and 80 blocks of Morrisania, we obtained 714 interviews in Spanish Harlem and 399 in Morrisania, a total of 1113.

C. The Representativeness of the Sample

Since indirect information was collected about all members of each Puerto Rican household visited, it was possible to determine whether or not our particular 1113 respondents were representative of the total Puerto Rican population residing in our sample of households.

As all our respondents were 18 years of age or over, we had to compare them to all household members who likewise were 18 years of age or over; thus, in the comparison of our respondent sample with the householders we had to restrict ourselves to adults.

However, all our respondents were Puerto Ricans who were born in Puerto Rico, whereas 109 of our adult householders were not born in Puerto Rico. Comparison of the results obtained by including and excluding these 109 householders not born in Puerto Rico indicates that the findings are the same—variation is less than 2 per cent. For example, including those not born in Puerto Rico, 44 per cent of all adult household members were male; excluding them, 43 per cent. Comparisons according to age are also similar.

ADULT HOUSEHOLD MEMBERS

	Male		Female	
Age	Including those not born in Puerto Rico	Excluding those not born in Puerto Rico	Including those not born in Puerto Rico	Excluding those not born in Puerto Rico
18–29	35%	32%	37%	35%
30–49	29	30	27	28
50 and over	36	38	36	37
TOTAL (100%)	(1293)	(1239)	(1676)	(1621)

It would thus seem that we did not bias our investigation by excluding those adults not born in Puerto Rico, and that we were justified in delimiting our household sample to those born in Puerto Rico.

Here are some comparisons between the 1113 respondents and 2860 adult householders born in Puerto Rico:

1. *Sex:*

Our respondents included a few more women proportionately than the householders: 63 per cent of the respondents, but 57 per cent of the householders, were female. Interviewing among a working population, this is one of the most difficult biases to overcome. Because of the large number of Puerto Ricans employed in the merchant marine, we were not able to reach many who were out on ships during the interview period. Rather than omit these households altogether (e.g., where a man in the merchant marine was to be interviewed) we took the next person according to our system of selection.

2. *Age:*

MEN. Through losing the merchant marine employees we also had proportionately fewer men between 18 and 29 among our respondents than among householders.

RESPONDENTS AND HOUSEHOLDERS BY AGE AND SEX

Age	Male		Female	
	Respondents	Householders	Respondents	Householders
18-29	27%	32%	31%	35%
30-49	33	30	31	28
50 and over	40	38	38	37
TOTAL (100%)	(417)	(1239)	(696)	(1621)

WOMEN. Again we had 4 per cent fewer female respondents between 18 and 29 years than among householders, which also reflects the difficulties in reaching the working population—many we had to give up because they could not be reached at home. It should be noted that we substituted another household member *only* in the cases of the merchant marine worker at sea.

3. *Time of Arrival:*

We had fewer recent arrivals among the women respondents.

RESPONDENTS AND HOUSEHOLDERS, BY TIME OF MIGRATION AND SEX

Time of arrival	Male		Female	
	Respondents	Householders	Respondents	Householders
1946-48	27%	28%	24%	30%
1940-45	25	26	26	27
1930-39	16	16	23	21
1929 or earlier	32	30	27	22
TOTAL (100%)	(417)	(1149)	(696)	(1570)

4. *Labor Force Status:*

Four per cent fewer male and female respondents were in the labor force then working for pay than householders. As a result, there was a slight overemphasis on relief cases, arising partly from the selective nature of the refusals to be interviewed. It was the impression of the interviewers that most of the refusals came from families which had risen on the economic and status scale and no longer identified themselves with the migrant group.

RESPONDENTS AND HOUSEHOLDERS, BY EMPLOYMENT STATUS AND SEX

	Male		Female	
Employment Status	*Respondents*	*Householders*	*Respondents*	*Householders*
Working for pay	75%	79%	36%	40%
Unemployed, seeking work	9	9	3	4
Unpaid family worker	—	—	2	3
Unemployed, ill	4	4	3	3
Relief	7	4	12	8
Housewife	—	—	42	40
Student	3	2	—	—
Retired, pensioned	2	2	2	2
TOTAL (100%)	(416)	(1257)	(680)	(1644)

5. *Occupation and Industry:*

Our sample accurately represented the occupation and industry of the householders in the labor force with the exception of the underrepresentation of the men in the merchant marine, which resulted in an overrepresentation of service workers.

RESPONDENTS AND HOUSEHOLDERS, BY OCCUPATION AND SEX

	Male		Female	
Occupational Level	*Respondents*	*Householders*	*Respondents*	*Householders*
"White collar"	15%	15%	9%	10%
Handworkers	85	85	91	90
TOTAL (100%)	(362)	(826)	(248)	(616)

RESPONDENTS AND HOUSEHOLDERS, BY SEX AND INDUSTRY

Industry	Male		Female	
	Respondents	Householders	Respondents	Householders
Wholesale and retail trade	5%	6%	2%	2%
Government	3	3	—	1
Professional service	2	1	1	1
Processing, manufacturing, construction	38	39	76	77
Merchant marine, shipping	7	11	—	—
Home industry	—	—	1	1
Service and domestic service	43	39	20	18
Amusement	2	1	—	—
TOTAL (100%)	(313)	(916)	(240)	(596)

6. *Income:*

Our respondents had a higher income than the householders, probably due to the undercount of young people and recent arrivals who would have lower incomes.

RESPONDENTS AND HOUSEHOLDERS, BY WEEKLY EARNINGS AND SEX

Weekly Earnings	Male		Female	
	Respondents	Householders	Respondents	Householders
$60 and over	17%	13%	2%	2%
$50–$59	16	13	6	4
$40–49	28	26	16	17
$30–$39	31	37	44	42
$20–$29	7	10	25	29
Less than $19	1	1	7	6
TOTAL (100%)	(360)	(927)	(247)	(649)

Examination of these comparisons seems to reveal that the 1113 respondents we selected from the 2860 adult householders born in Puerto Rico are tolerably representative. Our sample appears to under-represent slightly the males, the most recent arrivals among the women, the youngest age group, the proportion in the labor force, and the lower income group. These differences, however, appear to be so slight that they do not seriously threaten the reliability of the type of statistical statements we have made on the basis of this sample.

Index I

Ethnic Minorities, P. R., image of treatment of, 135-36, 200

Expectations, occupational, 159-61; striving and, 167-69; educational, for self and children, 166-67

Family, structure in N. Y., 95-99; in P. R., 8-10

Friendships, in N. Y., 100-05

Goldsen, R. K., x

Hanson, A. C., 176

Hibben, T., 177, 184

Hourwich, I. A., 192

Housing, in N. Y., 92-95

Howell, B., 175

Illegitimacy, in P. R., 9

Income, per capita, in N. Y., 94-95; in P. R., 18-19

Information, and migration, 53-56

Intention to remain in N. Y., leadership and, 57-59; original and present, 47-48

Isaac, J., 178

Isales, C., x

Janer, J., 175

Jerome, H., 186

Kevitt, B., x

Kinship in P. R., 8-10

Labor Unions, Puerto Ricans and, 109-10

Lait, J., 192

Language, assimilation and, 136-38; education and, in P. R., 11-12; proficiency and conspicuousness, 141-45—and family relations, 98-99—and "troubles," 146, 203—and public use of English, 143-44, 200-02; solidarity and, 137-38

Lawrence, R., x

Leadership, decision to migrate and, 46; information on migration and, 54-56, 186; intention to remain in N. Y. and 48-49, 57-59; reasons for migration and, 50-53

Lohmann, A., x

Magazine, reading in N. Y., 120

Marcantonio, V., 109

Marital status, composition of migrants, 29-30, 181

Marriage, common-law in P. R., 10

Mass communication media, exposure, 120-21, 196; magazines, 120; movies, 119; newspapers, 118-19; radio, 117-18

McKay, C., 194

McKay, H. D., 193

Mencken, H. L., 193

Migrant, industrial history of the, 34-38, 184; intentions to remain in N. Y., 57-59; social characteristics, 25-33, 38-39—age, 28-29—education, 30-32, 182-83— marital status, 29-30, 181—race, 26- 27, 180—sex, 25-26, 180—urban origin, 32-34, 182

Migration, American reaction to, 82-84; pattern of, 32-34, 56-57; population pressures in P. R. and, 19-21; rate, 24-25; reasons for, 49-53

Miller, R. A., 194

Miller, H. A., 195, 196

Mills, R. H., x

Mills, C. Wright, xi, 67

Mobility, See Occupational Mobility

Mortimer, L., 192

Motivation, business cycle and, 43-45; information and, 53-56; leadership and, 45-49; push-pull, 51-53; to remain, 57-59

Movie, attendance in N. Y., 119

Neighborhood, P. R., in N. Y., 99-100

Newspaper, reading in N. Y., 118-19

New York City, attraction for migrants, 49-53, 56, 187

Norms, adaptation and, 139-41

Occupation, preferred, and educational aspirations for sons, 164-65; and present, 158-59. See also Employment

Occupational, aspirations, for children, 161-67—for self, 157-59; characteristics of migrants, 34-38, 184; concentration, in industry, 68, 189—in N. Y., 66-68—in P. R.,

66; expectations, 159-61; level, adaptation and, 148; mobility, 68-73, 190-91—assimilation, 85-86—organizational membership, 106; striving, 167-69
Organization, Membership in N. Y., 105-10
Otero, P. M., 171, 172, 177

Packard, W. E., 173
Padilla, E., x
Park, R. E., 194, 195, 196
Payne, E. G., 84, 194
Pedreira, A. S., 171
Perez, M., 171, 172, 176
Perloff, H. S., 173, 184
Pico, R., 177, 184
Pinero, J. T., 172
Political, activity in N. Y., 108-09, 195; administration, of P. R., 13-16
Population, pressures in P. R. and migration, 19-21
Predisposition, to adapt, 152-55, 203-204
Psychic Contentment, adaptation and, 140-41, 146, 153
Puerto Rico, Ch. 1; Administration, 13-16; agriculture, 16-19; density, 3; edcuation, 10-13; family structure, 8-10; population, 19-21; Spanish heritage in, 3-6; status hierarchy, 6-8
Puerto Rican world in N. Y., Ch. 6; communities, 122-24; exposure to mass media, 118-21; family structure, 95-99; friendships, 100-05; housing, 92-95; neighborhood, 99-100; organizational membership, 105-10; "troubles," 114-17

Race, adaptation and, 152; assimilation and, 87, 132-36; attitude toward religion and, 113-14; composition of migrants, 26-27, 180; consciousness in P. R., 7-8; educational level of migrants and, 32; employment status and, 65-66; friendships and, 104; image of American attitude and, 127-29, 131, 197; intention to remain in N. Y. and, 49; mixture in P. R., 4-5; occupational level, wages and,

74-75—mobility and, 71-72; "troubles," and, 115
Radio, listening in N. Y., 117-18
Relief, orientations toward, 144-45
Religion, attitude toward, 112-13; church attendance and, 111; in N. Y., 110-14. See also Church
Research Design, viii-ix
Reuter, E. B., 171, 196
Rhetoric of Migration, 79-81, 84, 85
Roberts, L. J., 175
Rosario, C., x

Saveth, E. N., 192
Saxon, G., 194
Senior, C., x, 177, 185
Senior, R., x
Sereno, R., 171
Sex, adaptation and, 150-51; aspirations, expectations, striving and, 167-68; assimilation and, 87-90; attitude toward religion and, 113; church attendance and, 111-13; composition of migrants and, 25-26, 180; decision to migrate and, 45-46; educational level of migrants and, 32; employment, expectations in N. Y. and, 60-62—status, adaptation and, 147-48; family structure in N. Y. and, 95-97—in P. R. and, 8-10; friendships and, 102; image of American attitude and, 127, 129, 131, 197; intention to stay in N.Y. and, 48-49; labor force status in N. Y. and, 63-66; occupation in P. R. and, 34-38; occupational concentration and, 66-68—level, adaptation and, 148—wages and, 74-75—mobility and, 69-73—preferences and, 157-58; organizational membership and, 105-06; reasons for migration and, 50
Shaw, C. R., 193
Siegel, M., 172
Smith, T. L., 181
Social structure, P. R. in N. Y., Ch. 6; See The Puerto Rican World
Solidarity, Ch. 7; language and, 137-138
Spanish Heritage, ethnic prejudice in, 130; in P. R., 4-6

Index II: List of Tables